Carlos
Aldama's
Life in Batá

Carlos Aldama's Life in Batá

Carlos Aldama

INDIANA UNIVERSITY PRESS

Cuba, Diaspora, and the Drum

Umi Vaughan

Bloomington & Indianapolis

This book is a publication of

INDIANA UNIVERSITY PRESS
601 North Morton Street
Bloomington, Indiana 47404-3797 USA

iupress.indiana.edu

Telephone orders 800-842-6796
Fax orders 812-855-7931

Manufactured in the
United States of America

Library of Congress
Cataloging-in-Publication Data

Vaughan, Umi.
    Carlos Aldama's life in batá :
Cuba, diaspora, and the drum / Umi
Vaughan and Carlos Aldama.
    p. cm.
    Includes bibliographical
references and index.
    ISBN 978-0-253-35719-9 (cloth : alk.
paper) – ISBN 978-0-253-22378-4 (pbk.
: alk. paper) – ISBN 978-0-253-00567-0
(e-book) 1. Batá music – Cuba – History
and criticism. 2. Santeria music – History
and criticism. 3. Aldama, Carlos.
I. Aldama, Carlos. II. Title.
    ML1038.B38V38 2012
    786.9097291 – DC23
                                    2011028386

1 2 3 4 5   17 16 15 14 13 12

PAGE i
Carlos Aldama (foreground) plays batá,
2010. Photo by the author.

A mi maestro Jesús Pérez
y a todos los tamboleros
habidos y por haber
que aman este tambor batá

To my teacher Jesús Pérez
and all the drummers
past, present, and future
who love batá

CA

For my son Rumi,
and all the singers, dancers,
and drummers

Para mi hijo Rumi,
y todos los cantadores, bailadores,
y tamboleros

UV

Echu o Elegbara e
Elegbara moforibale
Elegba ago

Echu is the owner of vital force
Elegbara, I salute you
Make way

CONTENTS

FOREWORD

JOHN MASON

In his introduction to *Carlos Aldama's Life in Batá: Cuba, Diaspora, and the Drum*, Professor Umi Vaughan reminds us of what every percussionist, possessed by the spirit of the drum, must do – eat, drink, sleep, and dream drums. I have been a percussionist for forty-seven years and a priest of the òrìṣà Obátàlá for forty years. In the early years of my musical training, I would fall asleep in my bed while playing a drum, much to the annoyance of my very understanding parents. Even today, no tabletop is safe from my constant practicing. Just ask my wife.

Although the Africans in Cuba were able to reconstruct and invent innumerable musical instruments to represent and assist in cultural reclamation, the sacred set of three bàtá drums of the Yorùbá/Lùkùmí can unequivocally be considered the most important musical symbol of the reclamation movement. For the Yorùbá/Lùkùmí, the spirit that animates all drums is called *Àyàn* (The Chosen) and the drummers consecrated to that spirit are called *ọmọ Àyàn* (children of the Chosen). Like children everywhere, we all need good parents who will teach us about our place in the family history, show us the proper way to live in the world, and how to interact fairly with our fellow humans. For the traditional, religious drummer the discovering of the knowledgeable teacher who also possesses good character is critically important. The master drummer devotes his life to perfecting his art and learning to manipulate the transformative powers of the drum in service to the community. He must learn all the songs, praises, dances, and ritual gestures associated with each of the òrìṣà/divinities. Good character helps to assure the

ethical and prudent transmission of those transformative powers. Carlos
Aldama is widely considered one of those master teachers.

I first met Carlos Aldama in 1986 in Havana, Cuba, during my participation in *Folk Cuba,* a two-week long folkloric course hosted by Conjunto Folklórico Nacional de Cuba. He and Mario Aspirina were the two
main percussion instructors. I was told, without any fanfare and so didn't
think much of it at the time, that Mario came from a famous drumming
family and that Carlos had been taught by renowned drummer Jesús
Pérez, who was well known among informed American ritual drummers. Being a professional drummer and drumming instructor already,
I hadn't gone to Cuba to study drumming. In those days the *Folk Cuba*
course allowed American cultural researchers to go to Cuba without
problems from the United States government. My research goal was to
document, firsthand, elders, Lùkùmí history, and ritual procedures in
both Havana and Matanzas. So, farsighted, I missed an at-my-fingertips
golden research opportunity.

But it wasn't a total loss, because I was able to see and hear Carlos
Aldama play, in various drum ensembles, almost every day for the two
weeks of *Folk Cuba.* He was also present during, and contributed to,
an interview I conducted at the home of a famous singer, Ògún priest,
and Folklórico organizer, Lázaro Ros. Carlos even offered to give me
a private bàtá lesson, but I declined. The last time we saw each other
was in Matanzas in 1988 during Carnival. We were both trying, without success, to sit in and play with the world famous rumba group Los
Muñequitos de Matanzas. They performed every day during Carnival
on a public stage set up near the marina. Some time later, information
came to me that Carlos had come to the United States and was living in
Oakland, California. Another master had graced our community. I met
Umi Vaughan in 1999 at the University of Michigan, where I had been
invited to lecture by Professor Ruth Behar, who was familiar with my
works on Yorùbá religion in the Americas. Umi and I hit it off and kept
in touch. His artistic enthusiasm, intellectual curiosity, and thoughtful
respect serve him well.

Umi's finding and being accepted as an apprentice by master drummer Carlos Aldama was a blessing for us all. The title given to Aldama
when he was initiated as a priest of the òrìṣà Ṣàngó is *Ọba Kọ́wé(ì)'lù*

(Ruler who built enwrapped drums). This title seems to indicate that his life and story, spiritually tied to the initiators of the bàtá, may help those of us who missed the opportunity to study and spend time with him to fill in the missing blanks in our respective African drum-lore librettos. This book should urge us to ask Carlos and other living masters more questions, listen more carefully to their instruction, and record more of their great art and stories while they are still with us.

The term for drum apprentice, (ò)'yàmbóọkí, translates as "He who turned to beating greetings/praise." Professor Vaughan, compelled to turn his hands and feet to dance to the beat of the drum, has written a wonderful tribute that sounds out to praise his teacher, a master musician-historian whose lineage and biography must be closely studied because they spanned and impacted a very important period in both African Cuban and African American social and cultural history, and therefore, world history.

ACKNOWLEDGMENTS

Carlos Aldama would like to thank his mother and father, Jesús Pérez, and all of his old teachers. Thanks to Santa Torriente and Librada Quesada Mozorra. Thanks to his children: Maida, Dalia, Iliana, and Michel. Thanks to all of his godchildren (*ahijados*). Thanks to his life partner Yvette Phillips Aldama and to Piri Ochun. Thanks to Yagbe Gerrard, Michael Kramer, and Rick Ananda.

Umi Vaughan would like to thank Glen, Deborah, Yasmeen, Freddie, Jeffrey, Jeremiah, and Alan Vaughan, Secret and Ebony Onoh, and Nefertari Hawthorne. Thanks to José Francisco Barroso, Miriam Viant "La China," Victor Mendoza, Gloria Rolando, Nancy Morejón, Pedro Pérez Sarduy, Tomás Fernández Robaina, Miguel Barnet, María Teresa Linares, Olavo Alén, Carlos Moore, Rebecca Scott, and Ruth Behar for teaching me about Cuba. Thanks to Ifeoma Nwankwo, Kevin Gaines, Julius Scott, Kim Butler, and Yvonne Daniel for teaching me about the African Diaspora and for opening key doors. Thanks to Zeke Nealy, Ariel Fernández, C. K. Ladzekpo, Juma Santos, Otobaji Ngoma, Marcus Gordon, David Frazier, Teddy Strong, Sandy Pérez, Jesús Díaz, John Santos, Bill Summers, Sekou Gibson, Pancho Quinto, Enrique Mora, Papo Angarica, and Jesús "Cusito" Lorenzo for what they have taught me about drumming. Thanks to Janet Hart for her course on Oral History at the University of Michigan. Thanks to Ruth Nicole Brown for the initial push to begin writing this book.

Thanks to the faculty and staff at California State University Monterey Bay. Rina Benmayor, Maria Villaseñor, and Richard Bains offered great encouragement and made important suggestions. Annette March and Luana Conley administered a Teaching and Learning Grant that funded part of the work. Renee Curry, dean of the College of Arts and Humanities, generously supported the creation of the audio recording included with the book. Drew Waters engineered the recording sessions with student assistants Nick Rives and Jeff Mifflin, and university staff Cheryl Abbott, Yolanda Pérez, and Nicole Mendoza helped to coordinate it all. Thanks to Álvaro Gutiérrez (son of CSUMB professor Juan Gutiérrez) for his Spanish translation of an early draft of the manuscript. Thanks to library staff Rebecca Bergeon and Susanne Rodríguez for their help tracking down hard to find sources. Thanks to Troy Challenger, Barbara Beckmeyer, Jeff McCall, Aaron Roy, and Lark Simmons for help preparing digital photographs and maps. Thanks to all my students at CSUMB, especially from my class "Afro Cuba Hip Hop: Music and Dance in the Black Atlantic," who were a sounding board for some of the ideas presented here.

Thanks to the Alliance for California Traditional Arts for supporting this project through the 2009 Apprentice Program (especially to Sherwood Chen and Jaime García Leyva, who worked with us). Thanks to U.C. Berkeley doctoral student Lia Bascom, novelist Carolina de Robertis, Professor Jesse Hoffnung-Garskof (from the University of Michigan), and my neighbor Bob "Silky" O'Sullivan for their comments on the manuscript at various stages. Thanks to James Early and Daniel Sheehy at the Smithsonian for their positive energy and sound advice. Saludos to my compadre Joel "Machón" Mendoza and the two unknown drummers from Santiago de Cuba who appear in the cover photo.

Thanks to John Mason, Shukuru Sanders, and Oseye Mchawi for bolstering our communities with their work and for encouraging mine. Thanks to Calvin Holmes, Rick Ananda, and Taji Malik for drumming with Carlos and me on the audio recording. Thanks to Yvette Aldama for her trust and support. Thanks to Jane Behnken, Sarah Wyatt Swanson, Peter Froelich, Brian Herrmann, Louie Simon, Nancy Lightfoot, Jamison Cockerham, Ted Boardman, and all the staff at Indiana University Press who helped bring this book to completion. Finally, thanks to Carlos Aldama for teaching me so much about batá and life and for being a wonderful friend. *Muchas gracias, don Carlos.*

NOTE ON TRANSLITERATION

The reader will find here many words from the Lucumí language spoken in Cuba. It derives mostly from Yoruba, which is a tonal language spoken in the southwestern part of modern-day Nigeria. In Yoruba, tone or pitch is used to distinguish words, which otherwise share the same consonants and vowels; for example, *ilú* means "town" while *ilù* means "drum." Cuban Lucumí lost much of this tonal subtlety because it developed under the influence of Spanish language, which is non-tonal. Words in this book are spelled phonetically according to the conventions of Cuban usage.

TIMELINE

1400s   Batá developed among the Oyo (Yoruba) people
of West Africa (modern-day Nigeria)

1830   First set of consecrated batá drums created
by enslaved Yoruba in Cuba

188?   Pablo Roche is born in Havana

1915   Jesús Pérez is born in Havana

1935   Black scholar Gustavo Urrutia has batá to
play on Cuban radio for the first time

1936   Batá played by Pablo Roche, Jesús Pérez, and Águedo
Morales are heard in a public, non-ceremonial setting
for the first time at an academic conference organized
by Cuban lawyer/ethnologist Fernando Ortiz

1937   Carlos Aldama is born in Havana

1955   Carlos meets Jesús Pérez and starts to learn to play batá

1957   Pablo Roche dies

1959   Triumph of the Cuban Revolution under
the leadership of Fidel Castro

1961   First ever batá drum ceremony in the United
States (New York City), led by Julito Collazo

1962   Conjunto Folklórico Nacional de Cuba founded in Havana

1965   Carlos Aldama becomes the Musical Director
of Conjunto Folklórico Nacional de Cuba

1966   Guitarist Sergio Vitier founds Grupo Oru
with Carlos as an original member

1971   Carlos Aldama is consecrated as a priest of oricha Changó

1975 Umi Vaughan is born in Berkeley, California
1976 First set of consecrated batá drums reaches the United
      States (Miami) from Cuba with babalawo and drummer
      Pipo Pina. They are played in the first ever U.S. ceremony
      to use Añá, led by Julito Collazo in New York.
1980 Carlos's first trip to the United States coincides with the
      Mariel boat exodus from Cuba to the United States
1984 Carlos serves in the Cuban army's
      military intervention in Angola
1985 Jesús Pérez dies
1989 Fall of the Soviet bloc causes economic and social
      crisis called the "special period" in Cuba
1990 Carlos leaves Conjunto Folklórico Nacional de Cuba
1990–97 Carlos teaches percussion in Cuba, Mexico, and
      various European countries as an independent
      contractor, affiliated with Sergio Vitier's Grupo Oru
1997 Carlos travels to California to teach
      percussion for three years
1999 Carlos and Umi meet in Oakland, California
2000 Carlos is retired by the Ministry of Culture
      and leaves Cuba definitively
2004 Carlos and Umi begin extended batá study
2008 Carlos returns to Cuba for a brief visit

Carlos Aldama's Life in Batá

The Drum Speaks

* *Umi Vaughan* *

Añá unsoro, the drum speaks!
Tambó
The beat of life that always goes on
Percussive Spirit of Sound

All over the world
In joy and pain
People move,
People live, people love
To the beat

From Old Oyo to Old Havana
On to Brooklyn and Oakland
Where and what next?

There are meetings at crossroads
Beauty is born
Journeys come full circle
We celebrate the continuity of life
Through the drum

Moforibale. *I put my head to the floor in respect. I salute Changó by the altar, at the feet of Carlos Aldama (Oba Kwelu). Candles, coconut, and rum as an offering, to begin. "What do you want to learn? Do you want to learn to play a few rhythms for dance classes, or do you want to learn the lineage (la línea), the way of the drum?" "I want to be one of those guys that eats drums"* (de esos hombres que comen tambores).

[LISTEN TO TRACK 1]

Carlos Aldama and I felt compelled to co-author this book, *Carlos Aldama's Life in Batá: Cuba, Diaspora, and the Drum,* because his experience is so important for those interested in Cuba, the African Diaspora, and/or the batá drum tradition. Mr. Aldama's life experiences provide in-depth information that extends the more general works of anthropologists, historians, folklorists, and musicians. This book comes to light at a time when U.S. (and indeed world) attention is focused on Cuba due to recent political events. In 2008, Fidel Castro permanently relinquished direct leadership, which raised questions about Cuba's future in a post-Castro era; in 2009 and 2011, President Barack Obama eased restrictions on U.S. travel and cash remittances to Cuba, signaling his desire for reconciliation between the two countries. The consistent popularity of Cuban music in the United States, Europe, Latin America, and Africa over the past five decades (most recently with the Buena Vista Social Club, Chucho Valdés, Arturo Sandoval et al.) and the deaths of important Cuban musicians – some famous internationally like singer Celia Cruz or bassist Israel "Cachao" López (creator of the mambo), others less well known like rumba virtuoso Pancho Quinto or batá masters Regino Jiménez, Orlando "Puntilla" Ríos, and Francisco Aguabella – also lend a sense of urgency to the project. As a principal student of Cuba's old guard of ritual drummers, founding member and long-time musical director of Cuba's National Folkloric Company (Conjunto Folklórico Nacional), Carlos Aldama is a window into a world of musical knowledge and life experience during a *golden age* of Cuban Santería.

In this book, Carlos Aldama shares anecdotes that give insight into what life was like for an Afro-Cuban musician and his family before and during the Cuban Revolution. He explains, for example, that instead of a hospital experience, he was born at home with midwives that used African herbs. Carlos also relays the meaning and social function of the batá drums, and gives his personal philosophy on how to play, complete with technical pointers for musicians. He instructs, "If you can't hear yourself, then no one else can either!" For those interested in African American religions (like Santería, Vodou, and Candomblé), he recounts ancient stories as well. Carlos explains, for example, how the Ibeji (the sacred twins of the Yoruba) drummed the devil into submission and saved the world.

Carlos Aldama's Life in Batá is significant because, by telling Carlos's story, it reveals a world common to many black Cubans from his era, especially batá drummers, and practitioners of Afro-Cuban religions. Carlos's reactions to that world, told from his perspective, are his own and are also shared in various degrees by others.

CUBA

Nature seems to have destined Carlos Aldama's hometown of Havana, Cuba, to be an important stop in most travel between the Old World and the New – a crossroads. Even today Atlantic waters and wind currents push westward through the channel between Cuba and the Yucatán Peninsula until they turn northward in the Gulf of Mexico. Then the current sweeps along the Cuban coast and squeezes through the ninety-mile strait between Florida and Cuba, catching the great Gulf Stream along the American coast before heading back toward Europe. In the colonial period, beginning in the 1500s, Havana was thus a logical stop, an important transfer point for wealth coming from Spanish island and mainland colonies in preparation for the return trip across the Atlantic to Spain.[1]

While sailors, prostitutes, merchants, and slaves shared nourishment and entertainment, the native Taíno were quickly decimated by European disease, forced labor, and wanton violence. Thus early Havana culture was created by mariners of various nationalities (and races): enslaved Africans from various ethnic groups and locations who provided domestic labor, a limited number of European women who worked largely as prostitutes, and a growing mixed-race population, the offspring of the motley crew of characters constantly passing through.[2]

Africans came to Cuba starting perhaps as early as Columbus's first journey, and were an important cultural factor on the island by the seventeenth century. They became even more important with the massive slave importations of the nineteenth century that would make Cuba *the* world superpower of sugar for a long time.[3] Cuba and Afro Cuba have been part of each other from the start. Mandingo, Mina, Ashanti, Madagascar, and many ethnic groups arrived in Cuba; however, Yoruba,

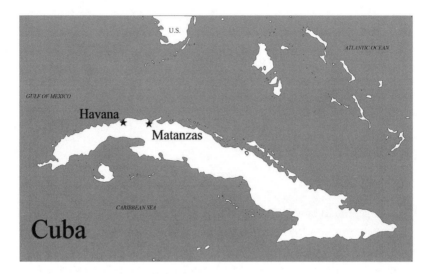

Havana and Matanzas are the main centers of batá drumming in Cuba.
Prepared by Barbara Beckmeyer, Aaron Roy, and the author, 2010.

Fon/Arará, Congo, and Carabalí/Abakuá cultures[4] remain most clearly discernible due to sheer numbers, time of arrival, and particular characteristics of the various groups.

The Yoruba (and other African) traditions in the island have served as an important element of cohesion, strength, identification, and pride, and have also become a theoretical and philosophical base for black Cubans in their resistance against slavery and then in their later struggle against racism.[5] The various elements of Cuba's black population evolved from diverse origins to a cohesive Afro-Cuban tradition that permeated not only the artistic and intellectual spheres of Cuban life, but also the social and religious dimensions as well.[6]

By the end of the sixteenth century, Havana was Cuba's capital and known as the Key to the New World. Over time, architectural styles, music/dance, religion, politics, and fashion have marked the originality of the city, even as it has mirrored Europe, North and South America, Africa, and other Caribbean islands. From its founding to the twentieth century, Havana transformed from a city originally designed and ruled by the Spanish, to one modernized by the United States, and, ultimately governed by a centrally planned Cuban government.[7]

Afro-Cuban heritage is an entire body of knowledge, experience, and values that is transmitted orally and through customary practice, stretching from the colonial era to the present day. It represents embodied knowledge passed down from generation to generation since colonial times. In the process a distinct Afro-Cuban culture has developed, which has been gifted with a popular imagination that is capable of substituting elements and adjusting philosophical values to new social situations with great improvisational virtuosity.[8] This purposeful transmission of culture under hostile conditions has sustained the black population of Cuba and enriched the nation as a whole. *Carlos Aldama's Life in Batá* affirms that Afro Cuba is part of Cuba's soul and that Cuba, in turn, is a key point within the larger African Diaspora.

DIASPORA

Diaspora is the diverse unity of a people spread far and wide. Originally the term came from the Greek word meaning "to scatter." It appears in the Bible[9] and, beginning in the late nineteenth century, was used for decades almost exclusively in reference to Jews who were scattered throughout Europe and North and South America. Later, in the 1950s and 1960s, the "African Diaspora" came to mean all those communities around the world with close genetic and cultural ties to Africa.[10] Thus "African Diaspora" refers to a transnational and intercultural multiplicity in which a "common thread [links] an infinitely wide range of manifestations."[11] The various cultures and communities within the wider diaspora are connected by 1) African genetic and cultural heritage; 2) the colonial/neocolonial experience; and 3) modernization/globalization.[12]

There are several qualities associated with diaspora: dispersal from homeland, often by violent forces, the making of a memory and a vision of that homeland, marginalization in the new location, and a commitment to the maintenance/restoration of and identity with the homeland that shapes the consciousness and solidarity of the group.[13] Diaspora entails continuity and connection; however, as Carlos's stories show, diaspora also connotes distance and the limits of complete identification. Diasporas are sentimental communities, but also habit communities reinforced by certain kinds of acts and events: home-style meals, religious rituals, drumming, and so on. Through these actions people restage the homeland in the new host location.[14]

Scholars have noted music and dance as pivotal aspects of culture and effective tools for social action within African Diaspora communities.[15] The movement of Yoruba people and the reinvention of batá in the New World, Carlos Aldama's travel around the globe and eventual immigration to the United States, and my own research in black communities in various nations exemplify these themes and trace several trajectories of diaspora.

THE DRUM

The family of the three batá drums is one of the richest cultural legacies that enslaved Yoruba people brought with them into the New World. Its rhythms have helped maintain religious and cultural practices shared by millions of people who are spread far and wide. It is important to at least briefly sketch the history of the drum, as a backdrop for everything that is to come, since this book deals with the performance of the Yoruba batá drums both in Cuba and the United States, especially the inventions and tensions inherent to the movement of the tradition between shores and generations.

The batá are two-headed, hourglass-shaped talking drums of the Yoruba people of Nigeria. The earliest batá tradition dates back to the fifteenth-century reign of Changó – *alafin* (owner of the palace) of Oyo, seat of the Yoruba Empire.[16] He loved and demanded the fiery, energetic, sharp, yet cool, seductive, and temperamental sounds of the batá drums, which became an important part of his legacy. In the nineteenth century, as the Yoruba Empire crumbled under the strain of civil war, and simultaneously the agricultural industries of the Americas called for more labor, the batá were transplanted to Cuba and adapted there by related enslaved African ethnic groups that came to be known collectively as Yoruba. In Nigeria, musicians stand to play the four drums that are included in the typical batá ensemble.[17] In Cuba, however, just three batá complete the set and the drums are played while seated. The largest and lead drum is called the *iyá* (mother). The middle-size drum is called the *itótele* (the one that follows). The smallest drum is called the *okónkolo*

Afro-Cuban Batá. *Lying down,* itótele; *large and with bells,* iyá; *standing on right,* okónkolo.
Photographer unknown. *Courtesy of Carlos Aldama.*

(the stutterer). All together, the tones of the drums recreate language to praise and tease or "call down" the spirits, known as *oricha*[18] or *santos* in the Yoruba-derived Afro-Cuban religion called Santería. Whereas in the Oyo area of Yorubaland the batá had saluted only ancestor spirits and Changó himself, king of the drum and dance, in Cuba they were reoriented to address an entire pantheon of oricha.

In Cuba there are two main roots of batá drum tradition – one in Havana and the other in Matanzas. Partly due to the high concentration of Yoruba slave labor on sugar plantations (*ingenios*) in both areas, Yoruba culture flourished in the northwestern part of the island. Ancestor veneration, oricha worship, and the batá drum were central. Because of its seclusion relative to Havana, Matanzas style is considered by many to be purer and the senior of the two traditions.[19] Matanzas is hailed by many as *la raíz* (the root), with worship specialists who can conduct certain ceremonies, for example, that are different from those in Havana and which are considered closer to Nigerian style (e.g., at times playing batá with leather straps as opposed to the open hand). Still, enslaved Yoruba also richly influenced the capital of Havana and it has retained Santería and batá traditions that are more widely known both on the island and abroad. For example, most batá players within and outside of Cuba play Havana style, which is the tradition that Carlos Aldama represents.[20]

HOW THIS BOOK WAS BORN

The voice you will experience most in this book belongs to Carlos Aldama. You will see that he is an intelligent, funny, wise, very Cuban man – *cubano, cubano* as they say. If you could sit with him he would surely intrigue and entertain you, as well as teach you something of what he knows. But the fact is that very few have the opportunity to meet Carlos or sit with him long enough to hear what they long to know; that is where my work, my role in *Carlos Aldama's Life in Batá* comes in. In this story I am present as *yambokí* (apprentice to the drum), interviewer, transcriber, translator, academic connoisseur, editor, and peddler.[21]

I am an African American artist and anthropologist who explores singing and dance, creates photographs and performances, as well as publishes about African Diaspora culture. I was born and raised in Oakland, California, to a dancer/choreographer and a schoolteacher. At an early age I was exposed to African-derived culture by my parents and was blessed to travel abroad with them to Mexico, Senegal, and Gambia. Language was always a strong interest. Starting with Spanish as a child, I went on to speak Italian, French, Portuguese, and some Yoruba. In 1996, during my senior year at Morehouse College, my mother traveled to Cuba and piqued my interest with her stories. I also met a dynamic, young folkloric dancer named José Francisco Barroso, who had recently moved from Havana to Oakland. I danced every Sunday in a free community class he gave at the Redwood Heights Recreation Center, and eventually danced and sang as part of his performance troupe Obakoso. I made my first trip to the island with him in 1998. Soon after, as a graduate student of Anthropology at the University of Michigan, I conducted research in Cuba about Afro-Cuban popular music and dance.[22] Based on this artistic training and anthropological fieldwork, I have created scholarly presentations, art exhibits, and cultural events in the United States and abroad. I seek to contribute to African Diaspora culture through rigorous scholarship and serious "hands-on" creative practice, including batá drumming. My training as a dancer/singer/drummer, as a photographer, and as a researcher culminated in my journey as a batá drummer.

I started batá drumming in Oakland around the time I began graduate school. Calvin Holmes and Sekou Gibson (both African American) were my first influences. Later I studied in Havana, Cuba, with Ariel Fernández, an instructor at the Superior Institute of Art. Otobaji Ngoma and David Frazier (African Americans) have been very influential instructors as well. I practiced many of the basic rhythms alone in snowy Ann Arbor, rehearsing with a videotape of Carlos Aldama. The same video still circulates as a common study tool among students of the drum. I first met Carlos Aldama face to face in 1999 when I paid him for the tape I had been studying in Michigan. I walked up to him and said, "You don't know me yet but I'm one of your students." We became friends later when he attended a party at my house in Oakland.

In the midst of about twenty African American and Caribbean party people, I watched Carlos preen and gently "stutter-step" the traditional Abakuá masquerade dance. These foot movements give the impression of a blind man tentatively, yet gracefully and rhythmically "tip-toeing" his way. The dance also includes complex gestures with the arms, legs, head, and so forth, that are full of historical and ritual meaning. They come from Abakuá, which is a male secret society brought to Cuba from the Calabar region of West Africa.[23] When I saw Carlos do this dance in the soul train line, I knew his presence in the Bay Area and in my life would bring a metamorphosis. In time, he would change my thinking about tradition and my place in it and transform the way that many batá drummers play.

I decided to approach Carlos for lessons at the suggestion of one of the Bay Area's long-time batá drummers, Calvin Holmes. Several drummers had been pressuring Calvin to give them lessons; but he always said, "Go learn it from Carlos Aldama, that's who you *need* to study with!" My one-on-one batá lessons with Carlos from 2004 to 2010 really began this book project. In our recorded *clases* (lessons) we documented musical learning and in the process exemplified the importance of master-apprentice relationships in transmitting musical knowledge and cultural tradition. I interviewed Carlos informally during our two-hour sessions, which usually took place on weekday afternoons. During the first years we talked mainly about issues related directly to the batá, but later, increasingly about wider concerns. Most recently, when it dawned on us how timely and important this project could be, we conducted themed interviews in order to clearly frame his life story. These conversations have resulted in an oral history.

Our work belongs to the tradition of "oral histories" or "life stories" that are created through a dialogic process.[24] Like Cuban ethnologist Miguel Barnet and Estéban Montejo, who produced *Biography of a Runaway Slave,* and like sociologist Barry Levine and Benjy Lopez, who made *Reflections on a Puerto Rican Life,* Carlos and I created this work through an extended "toma y dame," or give and take. I helped generate Carlos's narrative with my questions: "Why did you choose to play the drum? How did you learn? What songs go with this rhythm? When do I come in? I don't understand yet..." My laughter, my silence, my fascination, and my finger on the audio recorder influenced Carlos's story. The drums took part in our conversation too, as particular *toques* conjured people, events, and emotions out of Carlos's past and into this book.

In transcribing our work I have attempted to render Carlos's voice as I was hearing it through my tape recorder, and as it registered within me (how it made me feel). I have listened and re-listened to the tapes many times in the car as I drove around my home in Oakland or back and forth to my teaching post at California State University in Monterey Bay, generally a comfortable two-hour drive. First I listened to learn and practice the rhythms, focusing on Carlos's historical and philosophical explanations of where, when, and how a certain rhythm should be played. Later I listened before my computer screen as I worked on the transcriptions, focusing on the stories he told me of the setting in which he learned the drum and the men and women who taught him. After a time I memorized many tapes word for word, drum lick for drum lick.

In her excellent work about another Cuban drummer, Felipe García Villamil, María Teresa Vélez purposefully renders his voice in "standard English." She follows common practice for quoting informants in the anthropological literature, endeavoring above all to provide a "readable, understandable text."[25] This makes sense. It may be true that "One cannot have everything – the performance with all its divagations, and also an easily understandable story"; still, there is much to be learned from the sound of the original word, the shape of the story. [26] If we purposefully erase this "uniqueness" of the original telling I think we lose too much. There must be a balance. Therefore, I try not to tamper with the "essential qualities of everyday conversation and narrative and the subtleties and musicality"[27] of Carlos's Caribbean speech. Cubans of all classes and races swallow syllables and consonants and blur the distinctions between their *r*'s and *l*'s and even *d*'s. Linguists trace this characteristic accent to the Andalusian Spanish of the original settlers as modified by the difference between the consonant sounds of West African languages and Romance ones.[28] Cuban Spanish is Africa in your mouth: *ekelekuá, ahínamá, asere, moforibale, maferefun, aché.*[29] I leave many words in Spanish and *Lucumí* to allow Carlos's special Havana, Cuba, flavor to come through.

Some phrases are translated with an African American (English) swing, because, according to Carlos, it most closely parallels his feelings. (He would say, "From America I like *soul food*, that's it!") This allows for a more varied, "multi-layered" representation of Carlos and all he has to say about batá and Cuba than is possible through "straight" English. It also allows for more creative experimentation with language, inviting readers to *reach* to understand. There is a glossary at the end of the book with meanings for words and phrases that might be unfamiliar.

In order to avoid what Behar (1993) calls the disposableness of information, I have transformed myself in future chapters from a listener into a storyteller. All the information was gathered on specific dates and times, but these discrete moments have been submerged to help the story flow. I have had to "cut, cut, and cut away" at our six-year conversation to make it fit between the covers of this book.[30] Where Carlos speaks I have not added anything except for some explanatory endnotes; however, by organizing the story chronologically and through themes, by snipping and recombining, and by translating according to my own sensibilities I am present throughout the text with him. Like *Translated Woman* by Ruth Behar and *The Color of Water* by James McBride, *Carlos Aldama's Life in Batá* moves between the "novelistic" and the "dialogic" approaches to rendering life stories. Carlos Aldama speaks without much interruption; still we acknowledge the encounter/exchange that documented and transformed his experiences into text.

This is a polyglot tale that draws upon various narrative traditions to have its say. Whereas Esperanza's story in Behar's *Translated Woman* relies on the Christian narrative of suffering, redemption, Catholic confessions, and soap opera melodrama (*telenovelas*), Carlos's tale is grounded in Yoruba lore (*patakines*) and praise singing (*oriki*), as well as diasporic oral traditions like *signifyin'* and *playin' the dozens*. For example, while Esperanza tends to cast her characters as good or evil, Carlos does not use this either/or conception. Just as Changó is a deified ancestor portrayed as having both supreme virtues as well as serious foibles, important figures in Carlos's formation (such as ritual drummers like Pablo Roche and Jesús Pérez) are apotheosized yet remain quite human, imperfect.

ORGANIZATION

Since this book attempts to reconstruct the origins and trajectory of the batá and to articulate concepts that went without saying in the original context of our lessons, at the start of each chapter I provide short interludes before Carlos speaks. In them I offer possible interpretations of Carlos's stories, draw connections between his life and larger sociopolitical events and trends, and pose questions. By including these contextualizing sections I hope to spark discussion and establish a common ground for the various audiences that this work seeks to reach – drummers, *santeros,* scholars, and others.

The book breaks down into several sections:

In "Fundamento" Carlos and I set the foundation for the rest of the book. I sketch the evolution of Yoruba culture and batá in nineteenth-century Cuba and explain key concepts as a backdrop for Carlos's narrative. Carlos discusses the meaning of Añá and the nature of batá drumming, the role of women in ritual drum traditions, evolution/creation versus tradition/conservation, competing claims to authenticity, the relationship between Havana and Matanzas styles of batá drumming, as well as his account of his own philosophy as a teacher.

In "Learning My Trade" I set the socio-political scene in Cuba in the early part of the twentieth century, especially as related to Afro-Cuban religions and music. Carlos describes his family and talks about how he became interested in the drum, how he developed a relationship with the man who would become his teacher, and what the process of learning entailed. He explains important moments in his formation as a master drummer.

"Batá in the Revolution" is where I describe shifts in the batá drum tradition under the Cuban Revolution from 1959 to the present. Carlos discusses the founding of the National Folkloric Company (Conjunto Folklórico Nacional de Cuba), the organization of his musical work, his trip to Angola as a soldier of the Cuban army, tensions created by performing as a sacred/religious musician in the secular context of the concert stage, and experiments with musicians from other genres like jazz and popular dance music. Carlos retells important moments in Cuban history, like the Bay of Pigs invasion, the 1970 sugar harvest, and the Mariel boat exodus, from the vantage point of his personal involvement. In this chapter he also delves into the circumstances of his relocation to the San Francisco Bay Area.

In "Diaspora" I discuss the meanings and implications of that very term and point out tensions caused by the evolution of batá in the context of immigration to the United States. Carlos talks about his experiences as a musician in Africa, Europe, Latin America, the Caribbean, and the United States. He also shares his ideas about the differences between life in Cuba and the United States, and tells stories about making a living as a ritual drummer in a new country.

"Drum Lesson" is taken from classes that Carlos was giving to me during the course of the interviews. At the start, I reflect on the nature of our studying to prepare readers for what follows. Carlos further explains his approach to playing batá and gives tips for aspiring drummers. He discusses the importance of specific techniques and provides examples from his personal experience in batá drum ceremonies in Cuba and the United States.

In "The Future, What Comes Next?" I discuss batá pioneers in the United States before Carlos's arrival. Carlos shares his ideas about where the batá drum tradition will go from here. He reflects on Cuba after a recent visit home after several years' absence, commenting on changes there. He also considers the possibilities for Cuban music and musicians on the island and in the diaspora into the future.

In "Conclusion: The Drum Speaks Again" I position this book as a contribution in the ongoing struggle to maintain the batá drum tradition and uplift the people of the African Diaspora, and I point out new directions for future research.

Carlos Aldama's Life in Batá is a unique testament to how the contours of an individual life reflect and influence larger historical events and trends. It also exemplifies one interesting way to weave a life history text from the shared experience between master and apprentice. With this work Carlos and I hope to contribute to the continued *life* of this beautiful African tradition gone global.

Dide. *Rise up, I give you my blessing. A conversation begins and another* yambokí *takes the first step on the path to becoming a drummer.*

1

Fundamento

* Umi *

Batá drumming is used to support Afro-Cuban Santería. Santería is a "danced religion" based on Yoruba religious concepts disguised under and influenced by Catholic ideology and symbols. The foundation of Santería was established during the colonial period; subsequent developments in Cuba and other reaches of the diaspora, like California, are evolutions from this base. The original development began with the increased importation of enslaved Africans after 1762, when the British briefly occupied the island and opened it to trade more than ever before. The development of Santería took off even more in the early decades of the nineteenth century, when Cuba moved to replace Haiti (whose economy was destroyed by the only slave revolt to establish a black nation in the Americas) as the world's largest sugar producer. To do so Spanish Cuban planters brought more African labor to work the cane fields and refining machinery. Concurrent civil strife among the several Yoruba groups of West Africa resulted in even more enslaved.

YORUBA IN CUBA

Large numbers of Yoruba from all ranks of society arrived in Cuba at a time when slave care (lodging, etc.) improved and a fairly even ratio of male to female as well as old to young Africans was established.[1] Their arrival also coincided with the last decades of slavery, which was abolished in Cuba by 1886. For example, from 1850 to 1870, Yoruba subgroups such as the *Egba, Ijesa, Ijebu,* and *Oyo* formed one third of all the enslaved Africans brought to Cuba. Like Salvador da Bahia (Brazil), during much of the nineteenth century Havana could be considered a Yoruba city in the Americas.[2] This situation positioned the Yoruba to preserve their own lifestyle (religion, music, etc.) and to mark Cuban culture in unique ways. The experience of the Yoruba in Cuba exemplifies both *continuity* with Old World African traditions and *innovation* in response to New World conditions.

Whereas in Yorubaland each subgroup had only self-identified with a local community, in Cuba they gradually developed a wider shared identity. They became an ethnic "nation" (*nación*) alongside, although distinct from, other "nations" of related yet diverse peoples who founded new, common identities in Cuba.[3] In Yoruba language "olukumi" means "my friend"; as colonial officials heard this greeting they began to identify the Africans who used it by the same term. So it is that the name for the Yoruba nation in Cuba became Lucumí.

Lucumí ethnic identity in Cuba is closely related to Yoruba culture from Africa and forms one of the main bases for the Santería religion. Some people refer to Santería as "Lucumí religion" or "Lucumí." Santería is dominated by Yoruba traits and the ritual language used in Santería prayers, chants, and songs is dominated by Yoruba vocabulary and Yoruba phonetic and syntactic structures.[4] There has been influence from Catholicism and Kardecian Spiritism, but the foundation is Yoruba. "Fundamento" means the root of Lucumí identity, which first developed in nineteenth-century Cuba. It has inherent power, which is passed down from generation to generation through various ritual objects, social organizations, and activities. The crafted and consecrated batá themselves, groups of batá drummers and associated lineages, and communal religious celebrations with music are examples. Based on *fundamento,* the national ethnic designation of Lucumí came to describe distinct language, cultural attributes, physical characteristics, and ways of behaving. Like Carlos, many in Cuba are direct descendants of Yoruba.

At the same time, those who were not Yoruba by blood could become part of the Lucumí "nation." The gradual disappearance of African-born blacks in Cuba after slave importations ceased, intermarriage across ethnic groups, and religious conversion of non-Yoruba and even white

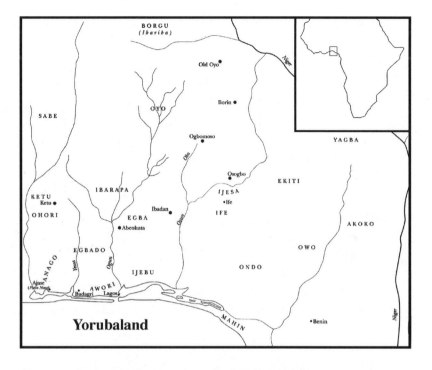

Regions throughout Yorubaland reflect the various subgroups that together founded the
Lucumí nation in Cuba. The city of Old Oyo in the north was the seat of the Yoruba Empire.
Prepared by Barbara Beckmeyer, Lark Simmons, and the author, 2010.

Cubans forced the tradition to expand or perish.[5] The Lucumí "nation"
became detached from the ethnic group that had developed it and took
on a life of its own.[6] Being Lucumí "began to rest less on [one's] ethnic
descent . . . than on the spiritual path [one] followed."[7] This greater inclu-
siveness allowed Lucumí tradition to survive and to this day facilitates its
spread. People in several locations around the world, with and without
connections of family descent, consider themselves to be "Yoruba." In
Nigeria, the batá drum is an important symbol of Yoruba identity. Fittingly, the Afro-Cuban batá tradition as described by Carlos Aldama is
one of the most powerful markers of Yoruba-Lucumí identity in Cuba
and everywhere it has spread.

The Lucumí of Cuba are part of what anthropologist J. Lorand Matory has called the Yoruba Diaspora. He contends that the Yoruba Diaspora consists of all the peoples that practice Yoruba-derived culture.

Communities in different regions like Nigeria, Brazil, Cuba, Puerto Rico, and the United States share common historical and spiritual roots. Furthermore, these communities are aware of and influence each other's religious practices.[8] Edwards and Mason list ten basic beliefs of the Yoruba, which apply to Santería and provide a backdrop for Carlos's stories. The Yoruba believe:

1. There is one God who created and controls the universe and all that is contained therein.
2. There are selected forces of nature called *òrìṣà*[9] that deal with the affairs of mankind on Earth and govern the universe in general.
3. The spirit of man lives on after death and can reincarnate back into the world of men.
4. Ancestor spirits have power over those who remain on Earth, and so must be remembered, appeased, honored, and consulted by the living.
5. In divination.
6. In the use of offerings and blood sacrifice to elevate their prayers to the oricha and the ancestors [eggun].
7. In magic.
8. In the magical and medicinal use of herbs.
9. Ritual song and dance are mandatory in the worship of God.
10. Humankind can commune with God through the vehicle of trance possession.[10]

The oricha are specific forces of nature, selected to exist within God, which govern different parts of the universe. The deities are associated with forces of nature, such as wind, volcanoes, iron, oceans, and rivers. Oricha that will be addressed later include Eleguá, the oricha of the crossroads and decisions; Ogun, the warrior and ironsmith; Ochosi, the hunter and marksman; Changó, king of the drum and dance; Obatalá, oricha of wisdom and peace; Oyá, warrior woman who controls the wind and the cemetery; Yemayá, goddess of the sea, mother of all; Ochun, oricha of sensuality, creativity, and fertility; and Orula, diviner par excellence.[11] Beyond their distinct symbolic representations, the oricha are fountains of vital spiritual energy that rejuvenate, sustain, and regulate the community. Santería is also referred to as La Regla de Ocha (The Law of the Oricha).

In Yorubaland Àyàn or Àyòn is the oricha of drums. In Cuba it is spelled Añá, yet pronounced exactly as it would be in Yorubaland. It is also the name of the African Satinwood tree, *Distemonanthus,* used to construct drums, Şàngó dance clubs, house posts, and sometimes canoes.[12] *Añá,* the godly energy that inhabits the drums, can be described as the Spirit of Sound that is able to invoke the deities and stir all the human emotions. In Yorubaland, Añá family lineages pass on performance and ritual knowledge from father to son.[13] In Cuba, the transmission by family lineage did not survive slavery and was replaced by batteries or groups of drummers led by a master drummer patriarch. As in Yorubaland, the father/teacher transmits his knowledge to and confers some of his status upon the son/apprentice.

Batá drums that possess Añá are said "to have *fundamento*" or "to be *de fundamento,*" meaning of or from the foundation. This translation of a Yoruba concept into Spanish underscores the association of batá with the core of Lucumí identity. According to Cuban Añá tradition, sacred batá must be "born" from a previously consecrated set of drums. This is how the "voice" of Añá is transmitted, allowing a new set of batá to talk to the oricha. The older set of drums becomes the "godfather" (*padrino*) of the new set, and so lineages or families of drums arise. Batá drummers rely on these lineages to establish the religious credentials of their drums.[14]

In Cuba, the term that was coined for unconsecrated batá is *aberikulá* (*abèrínkùlá*), which literally means "the ridiculer rumbling splits open," or to burst one's sides laughing. It is a term of derision. Before 1976 all batá played in the United States were unconsecrated, a survival necessity that blunted the sense of sharp criticism that the term implied in Cuba. In both Cuba and the United States today, batá that are *aberikulá* are still used when the patron cannot afford to hire a drum battery that possesses Añá.[15] Another name for unconsecrated batá in Cuba is *tambor judío,* or Jewish drum. The term was used by Lucumí drummers in the context of a colonial society dominated by Catholicism to signal unorthodoxy and a pejorative sense of difference. Drummers in the United States almost never use this term. As Carlos and I got to know each other, he would at first only invite me to play when a *tambor aberikulá* was being given. The stakes were not as high. Only later, after we became friends and he felt confident enough in my drumming, did he ever invite me to play at a *tambor de fundamento*.

"Santería" means the way of the saints (*santos*), which are none other than the Yoruba oricha that were masked in order to keep the tradition in the hostile context of slavery. In order to appease Catholic missionaries, enslaved Yoruba found similarities between oricha and saints, and while appearing to worship the saints continued to worship the oricha. Also, as the African sensibility is more open than closed to new religious influences, they may have actually devoted sincere spiritual energy to these Catholic survival adaptations. When Carlos Aldama speaks of *fundamento, oricha, Añá, aberikulá*, and even *fiesta* (see below and glossary), he is using his Yoruba head.[16] In doing so he illuminates an Afro-Cuban world shaped by Yoruba culture in diaspora.

One of the most important social spaces where Lucumí identity, Santería, and batá flourished was the *cabildo*. The cabildo tradition came to Cuba from Seville, Spain, and was aimed at organizing social classes on the basis of mutual aid and religion.[17] In Cuba they specifically functioned to organize, receive, orient, and regulate Africans who were brought to the island according to various ethnic groups or "nations," such as the Yoruba-Lucumí. Distinct ethnic groups formed separate *cabildos*. Cabildos were institutions of social control that ultimately facilitated African cultural continuity. Located at the bottom of the social order, the cabildos gave the only opportunity (or at least one of the few) for blacks in the Spanish world to organize, whether in Seville or Havana. In Cuba, the cabildos "became indisputably the melting pot that enabled the cosmogonies, languages, musics, songs, and dances related to those systems of worship to preserve their life and significance."[18] Many scholars consider that cabildos "incontestably form the starting point for African Santería in Cuba."[19]

Cabildos were the principle organizations for the religious life of Afro-Cubans up until the twentieth century.[20] By this time, cabildos, though not uniform, held several elements in common: they claimed old African ex-slaves as founders, Catholic patrons, their corresponding iconographic *banderas* (banners), and saintly devotions enshrined in decorative *capillas* (altars), legalized *reglamentos* (constitutions), mutual aid functions, dual administrative and sacred hierarchies, dues-paying memberships, and double Catholic and Lucumí liturgical regimens and festival cycles.[21] Changó Tedún or Changó De Dun (Changó arrives with a roar)[22] in Havana was arguably the most widely known and important Lucumí cabildo in Cuba's history.[23] In 1900, reincarnated as the Cabildo Africano Lucumí, it celebrated the annual feast day of its Catholic patron, Santa Bárbara, on December 4 with a Catholic mass, a formal procession afterward, and batá drumming for Changó.[24] The history of the Lucumí cabildos mirrors the transformation of the Lucumí ethnic identity itself. Over time cabildos became socio-religious societies of mixed ethnic and racial composition, whose diverse members practiced what was emerging as La Regla de Ocha or Santería. Many batá drums were built and consecrated for use within specific cabildos. Much of Carlos's experience as a *batalero* was gained, for example, in the annual procession put on by a famous cabildo in Regla.

"Oricha houses" or *ilé oricha* were born out of the cabildos and developed as more independent centers of socialization and Lucumí ritual practice. Each *ilé oricha* is made up of a lead priest or priestess and his or her following of younger priests initiated within the house as well as non-initiated apprentices and believers. Currently in Cuba and the United States, the oricha house is the main unit of communal observance. Within them, believers "become" Lucumí through initiation into the priesthoods of the various oricha. *Ilé oricha* are the main sponsors of the batá because they hire drummers and drums to support important ceremonies with music.

The batá drum tradition is classical music: its repertoire has order, balance, and restraint, while conforming to an established and elaborated art form of historical significance. Yoruba (Nigerian) and Cuban musicians acknowledge batá tradition as the authentic authority in expressing core religious values within Yoruba-derived culture. Each drum rhythm is associated with a particular oricha or spiritual entity and many rhythms are played in a liturgical order as a ceremonial blessing in honor of all the oricha, but also for the faithful worshipping community. Each worshipper is connected to several oricha and thereby to several rhythms as part of the tradition. Carlos, for example, is related to Changó and

Ochun, his spiritual "father" and "mother." I am connected most closely to Ochun and Eleguá.

Throughout the book, Carlos refers to an individual batá rhythm as a "tambor" or as a "toque." In addition to any particular rhythm played with the batá, *tambor* refers to the batá drum itself as well as to the ritual-musical gathering where batá rhythms praise and invoke the oricha. When Carlos uses the word *toque,* he means a rhythm played with the batá, or the ritual-musical gathering where this takes place, but *not* the batá drum. The overlapping of some terms emphasizes the fact that in Afro-Cuban culture, as in many cultures of the African Diaspora, social gatherings are closely tied to music/dance performance. In this word play, the event and the rhythm become one. Carlos uses the Lucumí terms *wemilere* and *bembé* as well as the Spanish words *fiesta* and *toque de santo* to refer to the gatherings only. These parties are offered occasionally by devotees; sometimes to celebrate the anniversary of an initiation into the religion, to give thanks for blessings or requests granted, or to reverse bad luck. At the parties batá drums recite prayers to the oricha and accompany communal singing. Songs that invoke the various oricha are sung in loose order in the form of a treatise (*tratado*) to the accompaniment of various batá rhythms or *toques*. Songs change and rhythms shift to accommodate emerging circumstances within the *fiesta*. The *toque de santo* is festive, but it is no frivolous party; it is serious business as well.

According to Carlos, the main functions of the batá within these gatherings are:

1. *Saluting the oricha in the altar room.* The opening drum prayer is played before an altar or "throne" on which actual representations of and food offerings to the oricha are present. This twenty- to thirty-minute series of toques (rhythms) is called the *oro igbodú* or alternatively *oro seco.* In Lucumí "oro" means "tradition" and "igbodú" means "altar room." The drums recite Yoruba tradition before the oricha in the altar room. In Spanish "seco" means "dry," referring to the fact that there is no singing during this portion of the ceremony; only drums speak.

2. *Saluting the santeros outside during the oro cantado.* The next part of the ceremony happens in a larger space outside of the altar

room, often in a living room or outside on a patio. Now, instead of addressing the altar, the drummers perform short toques in honor of the various oricha and to recognize the members of their priesthoods who are present at the *tambor*. The drums perform these salutes along with the *akpwon* (designated singer) and the rest of the priests (*santeros*) and non-initiates (*aleyos*) present that answer his or her songs like a chorus in call-and-response style.

3. *Announcing and confirming new initiates to the community.* In order to become a member of oricha priesthoods, one must undergo an initiation ceremony called *kariocha*. In Yoruba it means to "put oricha on the head." In Spanish and English this becomes "hacer santo" or "make saint." Saint in this case refers to the Yoruba oricha.[25] One culminating step in the initiation process is for the new initiate, called *iyawó* (bride of the oricha), to be presented to Añá as well as to the wider community of believers. Carlos describes this "presentation" in detail in chapter 2, "Learning My Trade."

4. *Calling down oricha to dance, give advice, and heal people at the party.* The next section of the ceremony, which is usually the longest and most intense, is where drummers, akpwon (singer), and the chorus of community members together endeavor to "pull" the oricha down into the gathering to dance and heal. Anthropologist and novelist Zora Neale Hurston describes it well: "[The oricha] manifests [itself] by 'mounting' a subject as a rider mounts a horse, then he speaks and acts through his mount. The person mounted does nothing of his own accord. He is the horse of the [oricha] until the spirit departs. Under the whip and guidance of the spirit-rider, the horse does and says many things that he or she would never have uttered unridden."[26] At the end of the *tambor*, after these various sections, the batá perform a set of *toques* to close the ceremony.

Music historian Katherine Hagedorn usefully refers to song, dance, and drumming as "divine utterances."[27] One key aspect in all of this is improvisation. There is flexibility for singers, dancers, and drummers to interpret the standard versions of the dance steps and gestures, songs, and toques. In fact, they must do so in order to create the *fresh,* living energy that is capable of summoning the oricha. Only this way can they achieve status as effective singers, dancers, and drummers. The improvisation on gestural and rhythmic "archetypes" enhances the divine potential of the performance.[28] Carlos insists, "Pablo Roche never played Bajuba like his father Andrés Sublime. Jesús never played exactly like Pablo, who taught him, and I cannot play it like Jesús did. Each of us has an emotional, spiritual concept that is different . . . even though we are born into the same tradition of respect, love, and consideration." Based on the foundation learned from our teachers, we must create a unique voice and then speak passionately. In Carlos's words, "You have to play some adornments to stand out and let people know that you are there, *presente!*"

In addition to knowing and being able to perform many rhythms and rhythmic sequences, master batá drummers need to know how to make and maintain the drums, including mechanical repair and ritual care. To become a batá drummer requires years of dedicated apprenticeship. The maintenance of traditions such as batá relies on the transmission of information from person to person, from generation to generation. The various structures that are described in this chapter – *cabildos* and *ilé oricha* (mutual aid organizations and oricha houses), *wemilere* (ritual-musical gatherings), *toques* (rhythms), and *tratados* (song treatises) – were used to remember and reconfigure Yoruba culture in Cuba. Furthermore, they have been and continue to be used to extend Lucumí culture from Cuba to the United States, Puerto Rico, Mexico, and beyond. In the activities that take place within these structures, individuals bear the responsibility of caring for the *fundamento* (foundation) passed on to them by their elders. Carlos has cared for what he learned very well. He proudly considers himself a slave to the drum.

For me, taking care means not only performing batá according to the tradition of "respect and consideration" that Carlos has taught me, but also writing this book. By telling his life story, Carlos and I capture several fleeting moments in the evolution of batá with the understanding that time and tradition inevitably move on. We extend these moments so that batá drummers, santeros, scholars, and others might learn from them. The product is a link in the chain of batá tradition connecting the oldest ancestors with the unborn of the future.

*   *Carlos*   ***

THE THREE DRUMS AND THEIR RELATIONSHIP

Batá is a language. Old folks learned by oral tradition. Any toque for any oricha is speech. If you play batá just for yourself, without listening, it will never work, no one will understand. When all three drums play together is when you understand. It's the synchronization of the six *parches* (skins). You can't play just for you; it's about the three drums coming together.[29] Okónkolo alone, itótele alone, iyá by itself is nothing. All three drums speaking, accompanied by the song, and the people is what makes the magic happen.

Okónkolo

The okónkolo is sharp (*agudo*). It is the rhythmic base. If there is no security, nobody can play, and the battery won't sound good. The iyá player leans on the itótele who leans on the okónkolo for support. The iyá listens to the okónkolo just as much. And this gives the music stability. Okónkolo has to be strong. You have to be right there, firm, so I can feel secure. The *enú* and the *chachá* are important![30] All six *parches*. There aren't as many opportunities to play here in the Bay Area as in Cuba, or Miami, or New York. But still, when you play you should go all out – test yourself. Don't be afraid to mess up your hand, play hard and strong. Okónkolo has its function. Okónkolo is the base. *Ripiquetea*, it repeats a simple phrase: ki lak, ki lak . . . and everybody says, "Look at him go!"

Itótele

The agility of the *segundero* or itótele player is of the utmost importance. A sleepy itótele player *está matao*, it's like he's dead and you have to wake him up. He needs to be alert. When I play iyá I tell you what to do on itótele. But sometimes you boss me too. Because if the iyá player is sour and doesn't play with much flavor, the segundero can try to inspire him, wake him, you know, "Giddy up!" Because, as the segundero, if you move, you make me look good on iyá. The segundero is the bodyguard (*guardaespalda*) of the *mayorcero*. He covers his mistakes. Once an iyá player sees the itótele player adding small adornments to the music – as long as he doesn't do too much – then that forces him to play better. If you don't, people will say, "*¡Ay, por Dios!* Who's that on iyá?"

The segundero has to know all the calls for the iyá, so that he can come in with the right toque. Everybody has their own reference point. You have to relax or you can't advance. It's not exercise or strengthening. It's more of a meditation. It's mental. You have to swing and dance it, or it will eat you up (*si no, acaba contigo*). The segundero must be super-agile. He has to cover up the errors of the mayorcero. The iyá player might be messing up because he's looking at a woman's behind. The segundero uses adornments sometimes to hide those mistakes.

I like all the batá a lot (*todos me gustan con cojones*), but do you know which drum is my favorite? The itótele – because it's the most melodic. Improvising is important, because you don't want to always play the same old thing over and over again. You have to play some adornments to stand out and let people know that you are there, *presente!* You can do a whole lot, change up, play a lot of *adornos,* as long as you don't do *too much* and annoy (*aborrecer*) the other players by losing the flow (*la línea*). You played two or three cute things, now that's enough! *¿Hasta cuándo? ¡Ya, no jodas más!* Remember, the lower drum can't dominate the superior drum. Okónkolo can't dominate the segundo, and segundo can't dominate the iyá. The iyá is in control, so you have to follow. The only time you step out of that relationship would be to hide an error the mayorcero makes, that's the only time. Then it's right back in line.

There's something very important: you have to play segundo. It will teach you to do several things on iyá that otherwise you won't be able to play. You have to know itótele. I was watching you play the other day and I said to myself, "He needs to relax!" *¡Relájate!* Don't tense up. *Suéltate* . . . relax, because if you tense up you won't be able to play. You've got to let your hands go! I would suggest to you personally that if you practice, say, one hour a day, practice forty-five minutes on itótele. Use the rest on iyá so you don't forget, but play mostly itótele. Because if you don't really master itótele, it will be difficult for you to master the iyá (*te va a costar trabajo dominar*). Itótele, itótele, itótele. It will help you to play relaxed. That tension will kill your playing.

Segundo gives you *la medida* when it comes to playing the *mayor*. There are things with the *mayor* that you could learn easily if you played every day. You go to a toque to play, practice, sing, and dance. But maybe you meet a pretty girl and you like her. You leave the toque, that's it, "I'm gonna go have my way with her, forget the batá!" It happens, *de verdad*, it's true. (*Te encontraste una cabrona y ya, pa' la pinga, me voy con ella.*) That's how it is because I lived it, you know? But since there aren't many toques here, you have to concentrate on holding on to this stuff. It's very easy. Once you get it, that's it.

The segundero must have a strong chachá. It gives the music stability. Remember he has to be the most agile. Itótele is a beautiful instrument. I like it a lot. All three drums are melodic, but especially itótele. Make the chachá stand out. It's an important part of the structure of the music and a crucial support for the iyá player. When the drums aren't supporting each other and one has to carry another, the balance is off. That's when you have to strain, your hands bleed, and all that stuff happens. Why? Because there's no stability. Remember there are three drums, six *parches*, which must play as one.

Iyá

The iyá is deep, dry, and strong (*grave, seco, y fuerte*). All three drums are strong, but the iyá uses both hands at the same time. When you play iyá, remember you are the one in control. You run things! It is very important to signal the beginning and the end of phrases and conversations. Very important. The sounds are punctuation marks. The iyá player MUST use *punta del dedo* (the fingertips) as a support for the chachá to get a bright sound. Understand? Use your chachá on the mayor as your entrance point, *tu pie*. To play iyá you must learn to shorten things (*apocopar*) in order to conserve and manage your energy.

Level, speed, and strength is all up to you. If you play soft, or if you play hard I have to follow you. The batá have to find a balance among all three drums. In a ceremony I start smooth and spread out my energy, thinking always of my second wind. Sometimes, based on the energy of the party, the drummers might start to *sacar majagua*, to practice or experiment, because people are talking, not focusing on the drum or calling the spirit. When you move up and begin to play iyá it's because you've listened and learned all the parts by playing good itótele first. Don't try to play iyá without playing good segundo. It gives you *la medida*. You have to work on the positions and hand techniques of the iyá now, like *punta de los dedos* (see section in chapter 5 on punta de los dedos).

The *chaworó* is a necklace of bells for each head of the iyá, to keep away negative spirits. You don't use chaworó to play for the dead. The chaworó is born with Añá drums. It can be of any metal. Even gold. Back in the day in La Habana, street vendors called *curros* used to sell *carbón* (coal). They carried their wares on carts pulled by mules, which they would dress up with brass bells to catch people's attention. Sometimes drummers used these same bells to make the chaworó for their drums. We secured the chaworó by interlacing the strap through the rope on the drum. Jesús's chaworó was made of bronze; 55 inches for the *chachá*, 110 on the *enú* side. They were made especially for him. The chaworó ring and seem to speak as you strike the drum. You don't have to shake them.

AÑÁ, THE SPIRIT OF SOUND

Añá, the oricha of the drum, is a male oricha. When Añá takes to the streets it is *para contraversiar* (to find conflict, raise hell) with the dancers, the singers, and to attract the spirits with this commotion. When you want to bring someone you have to convince them to come. If you don't they won't pay you any mind. Añá is a devil (*un diablo*) like a *prenda* (Palo altar). So when Añá goes out, it is to struggle (*luchar*), to make war (*guerrear*). Every now and again Añá is fed with a male goat (*chivo*). Otherwise roosters are good. Some drums require, by *oddun*, that you light a candle and place it on the floor before you play. It depends on the particular Osain that each drum has. Songs for Osain are especially sacred to Añá, because Añá and Osain work hand in hand. To consecrate Añá you need a santero, babalawo, *osainista*, and a *palero*. You have to have the four most important elements: animal, which is the drum skins, mineral in the metal chaworó bells and the small ring that goes on all the drums, vegetal in the wooden bodies of the drums, and human, the drummers themselves. Drummers can be called *omo alaña* (children of Añá) or *hijos de Osain* (sons of Osain). Añá is related mostly to Osain. Of course Añá is related to Changó too, which is logical because Changó is the king of the drums. But Osain works closest with Añá.

The difference between having one's hands "washed" for Añá and being "sworn to the drum" is a matter of degree and depth. The hand washing means that Añá has accepted you as an apprentice to the drum; it gives you permission to touch the drum and to play. Only later would you be officially sworn. Your elders, the owners of the drum, would decide when you were ready. Before not everyone could be initiated, it was more exclusive. There would be a party for Añá where special offerings were made. When I began to study batá in the 1950s there were only five sets of *fundamento* drums in Havana. It wasn't like today, when there are forty or more sets and anyone with a little money (*cualquiera con cuatro pesos*) can get their own. The drums were passed down from hand to hand, generation to generation. This is in Havana; Matanzas is another story.

If you have *ocha*[31] made they have to let you play, even if you are not omo Añá with your hands washed or formally sworn to the drum. I can't explain why this is, but I have seen it happen. I don't know why. Sometimes people who were never even drummers became *Olu batá*, owners of sacred drums. These must at least have ocha made. Drummers/omo Añá must be *men* (heterosexual, *tienen que ser hombres*). Añá is not machismo. Drummers of Añá are not *machistas* (male chauvinists). Today, yes, there is more of an element of *guapería* and violence, drummers carrying revolvers and all this madness. With the birth of so many new drums, the youth has come in and taken over. A drummer, omo Añá, is welcome at any toque. That is, unless they have serious personal problems with the hosts or other drummers.

Unlike La Regla de Ocha in general, where everyone is welcome, Añá does not accept women. Añá is like Abakuá in this way; women are more accepted after living an upstanding life (*respetada, bienquerida*), after they have stopped menstruating, once they're elders, and even then they are not allowed contact with the *fundamento*. I make the same comparison with Añá. Young women who are menstruating should not touch the drums. Another reason is *la debilidad femenina* (feminine weakness).

Up until now I've never heard of any women playing Añá.[32] There have been performance groups like Amelia Pedroso's. Most of them learned through the Conjunto, except for Fermin's daughter. She was born into it. After starting at the young age of six or so, after her mother had passed away, she ended up learning to play better than her dad. She could play four congas at once and batá too . . . but when Jesús came around he would say "Hey" and she would stop. She respected him a lot. She could play better than Fermin.

Back in Cuba, in our battery when it was necessary to do a ceremony for Añá, only Jesús and Trinidad would do the work. No one else. Pablo wasn't around anymore so it was just those two. They would seriously feed Añá maybe once every year. This was a much bigger deal than the rooster offered to Añá before any toque. Here in the U.S. I've washed the hands of several drummers but have not sworn anyone.

THE NATURE OF BATÁ DRUMMING

Cleverness is your best tool. Once upon a time the devil was in control of all the Earth's fertile land and a great famine threatened the world. As a last resort, Ibeji (the sacred twins) challenged the devil to a contest: they would drum and he would dance. If he became tired, then people could take over the fertile land. If not, then all the people would die. One of the twins began to drum and the devil started dancing. Meanwhile the second twin hid nearby and when the devil wasn't looking, the twins would switch off on the drums. They played so furiously for so long that the devil couldn't keep up! When he could take no more, he had to let the people onto the fertile ground. Through their cleverness and the drum, the Ibeji saved the world.

Don't spend all your energy at once. You have to distribute it evenly and wisely. A little bit here, a little bit there. The same way the spirit is moving, that's how you have to move too. There are some santeros who get mounted easily when you play for their oricha. Boom. Simple. They surrender themselves (*se entregan*). But there are others who don't and you have to pull them (*jalarlos*).[33] With these types, what happens after you've spent all your energy? You have nothing left. So you have to move with the spirit. You have to find the key point for each person. When you find it, then you start to work it. And that's when things take off and the spirit comes. There was this one big dude, bigger than me, who used to dance for Yemayá. When you would see him coming you'd have to get ready, because he took all day to get mounted. They called him the fan man (*abaniquito a real*) because he always danced with a little ten-cent fan. You would keep your eye on him throughout the whole party. When he started to gesture with the fan is when you knew he was close.

The singer has to do the same thing. Hunt the santeros. Because this is a *contraversia,* a clash. You give something, I take it, and give back. You have to have *picardía* (cleverness). You have to create your own personality as a drummer. And you have to learn how to get where you want to go in the context of the drumming ceremony, that is, control the energy and bring down oricha. Another very important thing is the characteristic of the oricha you are playing for. Changó has his *nivel* (level); Ochun has her own, Yemayá, etcetera. You have to keep this in mind. Use the personality of each oricha as your starting point to play. Ogun is war, so you have to play strong. Eleguá is strong too, he's a warrior, but you must also give his toque a playful character. These are just a few examples.

Remember, drums are not played in order to have a party, but rather to make *ebbó* (sacrifice). Drummers should sacrifice to their head before ceremonies because toques usually have to do with *ossogbo* (negative energy), debt, or some kind of problem. That's why we have somebody come and do a collective *rogación* for all the drummers before a ceremony. Go out like a gladiator to challenge and defend yourself among the other drummers, dancers, and singers. Don't be afraid to hit the drum hard. It's not about mistreating the drum, but bringing out its sound, its voice. You have to really play. *Esto es un ring de boxeo.* (This is a boxing ring.) And there's always someone ready to announce your mistake to everyone "*¿¡Qué pasó, chico!?*" just to mess with you. There are always guys who do those things, not necessarily to destroy you, but to play around and have fun. The jokester, the loudmouth, *el hijo de puta* (son of a bitch). It's part of the everyday life of the drum. Añá goes out to rumble. (*Sale a pelear.*) The singer, the drummer, and the dancer are three fighting cocks!

CONSERVATION VS. INNOVATION

Adornment is adornment . . . it just has to be sweet. Pedro Aspirina invented the famous *repiqueteo* (improvisation) on the itótele for Chachalokuafun (RIN kin kinkin – boom). But the greatest destroyer (*destructor*) and inventor of rhythms of all times is Papo Angarica. Papo created a whole new style of batá. He used to say I couldn't dig it because I was "old," but that's bullshit, I just couldn't get into what he was playing. It's no lie! A lot of records of his, listened to all over the world, have toques I've never heard before. He created a rhythm they call *La Bomba, Explosión,* the I-don't-know-what. One day I just had to tell him, "I don't understand you, *asere*." I just don't!

I'm conservative, but this drum thing is a *toma y dame* (a give and take). You may be playing in a *fiesta* one day and see a guy you dislike, and *rrrak!* Right there you create something new to express that. You don't stay boxed up in a strict format. You invent something new that you feel, and it's beautiful. I can show you the *golpe.* But you have to put in your part too. You have to let yourself go. Once you know the toque, let it all go, allow yourself to create. That way you break the monotony.

HAVANA AND MATANZAS

I respect *los matanceros* a lot, but I'm from Havana. When I used to visit Matanzas, I would sit down sometimes on okónkolo with Chachá, the famous drummer, and others.[34] But usually I didn't even play, because we were more focused on Abakuá.[35] Arará is *matancero* and *brazileño.* They cultivate Dahomey culture in Matanzas. *Los matanceros* have their own way of doing things – playing, constructing and lacing the drums, etcetera. Plus they sometimes use that *chancletica* (leather strap), which gives its own special sound. I don't see them playing like that anymore, and I think it's a shame. Between Havana and Matanzas there was always a difference and a respect. In Matanzas they speak *Suama* (a dialect of Abakuá) like you can't imagine. They speak Carabalí and Brícamo too. After Matanzas, the folks from Regla and Guanabacoa were the strongest. There were things in Abakuá that you had to go to Matanzas to learn. In Añá it was different; the knowledge was more evenly distributed. We had Pablo Roche and others who really knew the tradition.

A lot of people think that *los matanceros* are the gods of Cuban folklore. But no. I have a problem with that. In Santería too. *Cállate y respeta* (Shut your mouth and have some respect). Don't come to me about you are doing this or that ceremony Matanzas style; I don't want to hear it. According to how the person sings, is how you have to play, because they go together. That's one thing that bothers me about some drummers in California; they always want to play Matanzas style when I'm singing, and I'm from Havana. They should follow me, but instead they do what they want. And they're not even from Matanzas; they've spent only a few days there. Don't try to cross me up with that stuff. . . I don't know how to play Matanzas style. People try to show off and say, "This is from Matanzas." No disrespect, but to hell with Matanzas! (*Pa' la pinga Matanzas.*) They have their gifts and so do we in Havana.

TEACHING

There are different kinds of students. There are students who get frustrated and angry with themselves when they can't get something. There are other students who don't learn because they don't study; they'd rather hang out and play around. These last ones I cut off. "Don't bother to come back, *chico*," I tell them. I really do. If I see that you don't love the drums the way I do, then why waste my time? (*¿pa' qué voy a cargar agua en canasta?*) No, no, no.

Sometimes drummers play what they heard (*por haber oído*). It's not that they've been taught. What's the motive behind it? Consistency, confrontation . . . you have to go to toques. I never like to mistreat anyone. I've had really bad students – *brutos, brutos* – where I've known that they'd probably never learn anything (*ni pinga*). But there's one important reality: vocation. Very important. My vocation as a teacher means I have to have patience.

It's not just about the money, Umi. I've played for a lot of people in this world. So one day someone will have to play for me. I'm going to tell you, *siéntate*, have a seat and play. Demonstrate what I showed you.

Doesn't matter if you have paid me or not, *no importa*. You came to me to learn. Without being *autosuficiente* . . . autosuficiente (self-important) means those teachers that envy their students, who don't want them to learn more or pass them by. I'm not like that. I know my level, though. If you ask how a toque goes, I'll show it to you. All of it, to the best of my ability. But the student will always be the student, *olvídate* (forget about it). I'm not the type who thinks he's God's gift to this earth. Fuck it! If you love this music, if you are going to take care of it, then learn it, I'll teach you. Because I know that you will care for it.

Take Kota, for example. The Japanese guy. When he started he didn't know much. But I would see him *allí, allí* working at it. And I had to give it to him. This kid is serious! (*¡Este chiquito está del carajo pa'rriba!*) He played clean and strong, so I said come on. Because I see him struggling, I can see he really wants to learn. Among Cubans I've had no students at all. Cubans who weren't already drummers in Cuba did not learn how to play here in the U.S.

BATÁ BETWEEN SHORES

What you feel, you have to express through the drum. If what you're feeling is divorced from the drum, then it's bullshit. It's not just you. You are one part of a group. You have to unify yourself with the drum you are playing, with the other drummers, and with the people. I can't play if I don't feel. I can't play unless I remember something (*si no recuerdo algo*) and hold that image in my mind. A collective of people: the drummers, the singer, the priests, *los sinvergüenzas* (the peanut gallery). It's all of this. It would be good if you recorded this.

Besides, you're a *santero*, you have *santo* made. You have to understand a whole series of things. In Cuba you can learn everything, or at least a lot, in three or four months, but not here in California. Folks don't play every day here. The ones who play have their public, *su gente,* understand? There are some that work according to La Regla de Ocha, like they do in Cuba. Others don't; they have their own ideas. For example, here we are not all "santeros." We have ocha made, but we are not all santeros. What do I mean? A real santero is a person who has initiated someone else (*ha hecho santo a otra persona*).[36] You have ocha made but you are not a santero. I have it too, and I am a santero, because I have initiated others here and in Cuba. Don't get mad, it's true! Like babalawos who boast, "I'm a babalawo" when really they are just *awo* Orula, because they have not initiated anyone else. The same happens with drummers.

Here there's not the same contact . . . Michael Spiro has his battery of drummers who don't play for anyone else, just where he takes them. Eric has his fundamento drums, which he just brought recently. Barroso has a set too, which he just brought. But there is not that strong sense of identification with the different batteries: "I am a drummer of so-and-so" (*fulano*). Let's study, Umi. I'll teach you what Jesús taught me. Let's go. But it's not that I want you to fight with anyone or separate yourself. What I want is for you to learn my era, my moment when they taught me . . . for you to use now, in your own way, in these circumstances. Tomorrow, as omo Añá, anywhere you go out there, they will ask who taught you. And I'm not the best. But I am a drummer, *yo sí soy tambolero.* I sacrificed a lot (*me jodí mucho*). I am a drummer. When they ask who taught you and you say Carlos Aldama it will mean something. And if it's the U.S., even more so. That's how it is (*esto es así*).

2

Learning My Trade

* Umi *

The important Lucumí institution of the sacred batá drums, with its specialized bodies of technical, herbal, and musical knowledge, and its guilds of drummers "sworn" (*jurado*) to the drum spirit, Añá, did not arrive in Cuba as an intact "tradition." On the contrary, the batá complex was recreated, disseminated through the urban cabildo networks of Havana, Regla, and Matanzas, and transmitted intergenerationally through descending ritual lineages of drummers. Cuban ethnologist Fernando Ortiz writes that, although the drums were known before this, the first set of "orthodox" drums, constructed and prepared according to ritual protocol from Nigeria, was made in 1830 in the town of Regla (across the bay from Havana) by two slaves, Atandá (No Juan el Cojo) and Añabí (No Filomeno García), now famous as founding fathers among devotees of the batá.[1] According to this history, these men were the first to establish *batá de fundamento* in Cuba. As Santería and the batá developed and took root, important individuals emerged to shape and codify the tradition.[2] Among the drummers mentioned as central architects of the Havana lineage we find Andrés Roche and his son Pablo Roche, who represented the second and third generations of sacred batá drummers in Cuba.

Andrés Roche played African drums so beautifully in Cuba in the nineteenth century that he was called Andrés "Sublime." Pablo Roche was born at the end of the nineteenth century and died in 1944 (1957, according to Carlos Aldama).[3] Pablo Roche is discussed in detail in this

book in the context of personal reminiscences, as is his most famous
student, Jesús Pérez. Pérez was born in Havana in 1915 and died there in
1985. The transmission of batá knowledge from Andrés Roche to his son
Pablo followed the tradition of father/son apprenticeship used by Añá
family lineages in Yorubaland. However, the transmission from Pablo
Roche to his student Jesús Pérez helped to establish a new pattern in
which a master-patriarch ran "families" of batá drummers as a fictive
"father." Carlos Aldama refers to Pablo as "the father of it all" as he maps
out his own drum lineage. He notes how Pablo was known as a tough guy
who would even "hit drummers [his students] who were grown men."
Through his pedigree as the son of Andrés Sublime, his own skill as a
performer, and his stern persona, Pablo Roche commanded the status
of master drummer and teacher (called *kpuatakí*) as well as father figure
within his cadre of drummers and within the wider Santería and batá
community. Carlos goes on to tell stories about Pablo Roche, Jesús Pérez,
Nicolás Angarica, Papo Angarica, Regino Jiménez, and other elders,
contemporaries, and rivals that illuminate the inner workings of the
Añá batteries that served the Havana Santería community in the 1950s.

Carlos emphasizes that, for him, learning the drum was never a
question of money, but rather one of dedication. He never paid cash
for instruction. His lessons were "in the street." He paid by carrying
coconuts, skipping dates with beautiful young women to re-tune drums
with his teacher, missing dances at La Tropical in order to be at toques.
He points to the good fortune of having many opportunities to learn and
perform and to his own tenacity as the main reasons that allowed him to
achieve high skill and status as a batá drummer. Carlos sees himself as a
dedicated artisan, more than as a virtuoso artist.

Carlos explains how drum batteries in Havana had old-guard players and newer apprentices, and each group had its time to drum during
the ceremony. The *oro* at the start requires precision. The drums recite
ancient musical language in the altar room directly to the oricha, so the
oldest, most seasoned drummers must play then. The second part, saluting the oricha priests, is lighter and newer players often perform. The
pieces are short and the rhythms less intricate. The third part, calling
the oricha to mount priests, needs power and stamina. Drummers must
summon the energy/violence to break people open so that oricha can

enter and ride them. This is the time for the young bucks, the thorough-breds, to play – those that are experienced enough to make important de-cisions during the ceremony, but young enough to set the drums on fire. The presentation of new initiates to Añá requires drummers with oricha crowned to play. This is a major concept within La Regla de Ocha: One must have "it" in order to pass "it" on. The last section of the ceremony, the closing, calls for the same drummers who started by playing the oro to play again. This symbolizes the continuity, the circularity of life. *Con Dios comenzamos, con Dios terminamos.*

In the midst of the important details that Carlos's stories illuminate about the batá tradition, he also shows that there are no hard-and-fast rules. This, in fact, is another key principle in Yoruba thought: just as des-tiny is chosen before the soul is born, it can be amended. Drummers who have not been consecrated to Añá are sometimes allowed to play sacred drums. Sometimes omo Añá without oricha crowned are allowed to play for presentations. Drummers, like *babalawos,* should not be homosexual or susceptible to possession by the oricha, but it happens.

Another important issue for Carlos is the interplay and tension be-tween fidelity to tradition and originality, the mandate to create. Talking about Pablo Roche, Jesús Pérez, and himself, he emphasizes the impor-tance of creating your own personality while respecting tradition. Every drummer had his own personality and sound. Similarities, when they existed, indicated a close affinity with one's teacher. Carlos feels proud that sometimes people would confuse his playing with that of Jesús Pérez or Pablo Roche. At times Carlos and other drummers applaud or reject the *inventos* (creations) of batá innovators like Pancho Quinto or Papo Angarica. In the end, it seems that the reactions of the community of *santeros* and the *oricha* themselves determine which changes are accept-able and/or become part of the vocabulary of the drum. If community members continue to hire certain drummers because the oricha con-sistently arrive at *wemilere* to dance and heal attracted by their playing, then it means their drumming is sweet and their style will impose itself.[4]

Diverse political regimes throughout the twentieth century have denigrated and repressed African-based religions in Cuba, including Santería. In doing so, the state has legitimized the traditional associa-tion between blackness and backwardness.[5] Despite the national creed of Cuba Libre (Free Cuba) that guaranteed liberty and equality for all, during the early republic (1902–33) some administrations actively sought to de-Africanize Cuba. (For example, by promoting immigration from Spain or the deportation of Cuban blacks to Africa.) It was still true under the second republic (1933–59), regardless of the acceptance of various forms of black commercial dance music as true representations of "Cubanness." This is the world in which Carlos and his teachers learned.

Carlos came of age in the 1940s and 1950s, during a time when Santería had achieved a considerable amount of development and codification. From its nineteenth-century roots in Yoruba religion mixed with Catholicism and Kardecian Spiritism, it had become a uniquely Afro-Cuban religious practice, with batá drumming as a central component. Even though many Cubans derided Santería and its batá *toques* as vulgar and/or primitive, La Regla de Ocha was growing, even among white Cubans. Some (especially upper-class) whites dabbled in the religion while others became serious practitioners. Carlos mentions that in Regla (across the Bay from Havana) the whites were "*santeros,* and everything else, just like the blacks." Despite the fact that Afro-Cubans had been massacred as recently as 1912 for defending their political rights, and despite negative attitudes toward and continued repression of Santería, there was the sense that things were opening up.

Afro-Cuban music styles such as *son, guaracha, bolero, mambo,* and *chachachá* were gaining space on the island and triumphing abroad. The surge took place in the context of fundamental change in the commercial music of nearly all Western countries, driven partly by technological innovation in the form of radio broadcasting and sound recordings, partly by the nature of capitalism itself and a desire to expand markets into minority communities overseas, and partly as a result of growing wealth and increased numbers of overseas working classes. This was the jazz age, the era of bohemian Paris, and the Harlem Renaissance, when popular music/dance styles like *tango, calypso,* and *samba* emerged throughout the African Diaspora. Music and dance served as a means of real and symbolic empowerment for those who would otherwise have no voice.[6] The presence and increasing popularity of these black styles created a space for at least a partial re-evaluation of Santería and other Afro-Cuban cultural manifestations. If not yet respected as world religions on a par with Catholicism, at least the African traditions were being chosen as objects of academic study and acknowledged as real ingredients of Cuban culture.

Some greater acceptance of Santería can be seen in relationship to a growing interest in Afro-Cuban culture on the part of scholars, artists, and laypeople since the start of the twentieth century. Cuban lawyer and ethnologist Fernando Ortiz was the pioneer of Afro-Cuban studies and wrote seminal books on various aspects of Afro-Cuban culture, including Santería and batá. His 1906 book *Hampa afro-cubana: los negros brujos* (*Afro-Cuban Underworld: The Black Witch Doctors*) regards Afro-Cuban culture as "criminal" and reflects the widely held view that elements of African culture like Santería, with its drums and trance possession, were holding Cuba back as a modern nation. Over the course of his long career, however, Ortiz evolved a different view and produced a massive body of work that emphasized how African influences, such as Yoruba language, cooking, religion, batá drumming, and so on, are key elements in Cuban culture.

There was a general re-evaluation of Afro-Cuban culture, which influenced scholarship and virtually all domains of art, elite and popular.[7] Wilfredo Lam and Nicolás Guillén explored Afro-Cuban themes through painting and poetry respectively in what has been called the Afro-Cuban Arts Movement of the 1930s. Through Fernando Ortiz's work, the criminalization of Afro-Cuban sacred practices was gradually replaced with "spectacle-ization," as he began to organize public performances of religious music/dance that was traditionally private.[8] In 1936, Pablo Roche, Jesús Pérez, and Águedo Morales performed in the first-ever public concert to feature batá drumming, organized by Ortiz at Havana University.[9] Carlos mentions that Trinidad Torregosa and Pérez were the drummers who worked closest with Ortiz as informants after Pablo Roche died. In 1954, the Panart *Santero* LP, an important landmark recording, featured singing by Merceditas Valdés, Celia Cruz, Caridad Suárez, and batá drumming led by Jesús Pérez. At roughly the same time, commercial groups like Sonora Matancera and Bebo Valdés experimented with the use of batá as part of secular dance compositions, elaborating on experimentation initiated by Gilberto Valdés in the 1930s.[10]

Still, even in the 1940s and 1950s, middle-class Cubans considered Afro-Cuban folklore distasteful. Researchers like Ortiz and others had to fund their own work. Most citizens of color attended poorly funded schools; a significant number never graduated high school, dropping out early to support themselves and their families. Those who managed to educate themselves and enter the professions received lower salaries than their white counterparts. As the stage was set for Carlos to enter, positive cultural impulses struck a delicate balance with the prevalent negativity surrounding Santería and other things African in Cuba.[11]

Does Carlos recall the 1950s as a golden age for historical reasons, such as the culmination of a long period of extended development of Yoruba-Lucumí culture in Cuba, the decriminalization of Santería (despite continued repression), increased scholarly and artistic interest in Afro-Cuban culture, and the nationalization of blackness in commercial dance music? Or does he feel this way because, afterward, he lost his direct link through his teacher and patron to a set of sacred drums and an authoritative lineage?

*   Carlos   *

I was born Carlos Lázaro Aldama Pérez on November 4, 1937, but they registered me for 1938 because I lived with my grandmother, and not with my parents and siblings. This was because when I was born in her house she really took to me and told my mother she couldn't take me away. All my uncles and aunts lived away in the countryside. They were *guajiros*. My grandfather had passed away about nine months before and she was all alone. "This sweet black baby is mine and he's staying with me," she decided (*Este es mi negrito y se queda conmigo*). My brother and my sister had been born in hospitals but I was born in my grandmother's house. Midwives delivered a lot of kids in those days. They were called *parteras* (midwives) and they would heat up water, send folks to get fabric, or whatever they needed, and they helped women give birth right at home. My mother didn't work. My father supported her, even though they were not married.

On my father's side they were descendents of Aldama.[12] He was the Governor General of Cuba for a day. In Havana there's an Aldama Palace located on the corner of Reina and Amistad Streets. This man was rich. A Spaniard. In his house he kept about fifteen women. The statue outside the place to this day has him surrounded by women. People would tease me by calling him a *puto* (male whore) and I would tell them "Shut up, I'm an Aldama." Since he was wealthy and the island needed capital they made him Governor General. When he was ready to sign papers and swear in, they sent him away, though, because he would have fucked all the women! [laughter] My great grandmother, Saturnina Aldama, was a cook at that house, understand? She had been born in Cuba of parents who were Yoruba. In 1868, when many slaves were declared free in Cuba, Aldama liberated his and asked them where they wanted to live. He set up homes for them wherever they chose. My great grandmother chose the town of Casa Blanca, just outside of La Habana, where the canal of the Bay is located, next to Regla. My great grandmother did not have ocha made. Not all the slaves that came from Africa were religious. Dionisio Aldama, my dad's uncle, moved to Union de Reyes in Matanzas and was able to buy property. Eventually they called him the Golden Ox (*el buey de oro*). All the Aldamas in Matanzas are related. One of my uncles even looks Japanese!

My father's name was Ignacio Aldama. His job used to be cutting leather for shoes. He was a Chinese descendent. People said Japanese, but it was Chinese. In the early 1940s, he worked in Old Havana buying and selling leather for shoes. Later, after the revolution, he also became one of the ten founders of State Security (Seguridad del Estado) in Cuba. Fifth Avenue and Fourteenth Street is where that was located. He had a diploma from Fidel himself recognizing his contribution. He's buried in a special place along with the other founding members. This happened because he got involved in the revolution, selling weapons and things. So when the revolution triumphed, they called him.

On my mother's side, my great grandmother was from Africa. They brought her to Cuba as a small child. She was Yoruba too. My grandmother had santo – Changó and Eleguá. She received just one or two oricha like in Africa, not all the oricha like in Cuba. She was initiated in a town called Álaba in the province of Matanzas. My maternal grandfather had fought in the independence war of 1895. He was a *mambí* (Cuban independence fighter). Since my mother, Atanasia Pérez, was not married, the government gave her his army pension. My grandmother raised me though. She passed away when I was fourteen or fifteen years old, and I went to live with my brothers and my father. And as a kind of punishment for bad behavior, I was made to work as a tailor (*sastre*).

Marcelino Montor, a Spaniard in Cuba, was the man who taught me how to be a tailor and how to drink. They have a drink in Cuba called *España en Llama* (Spain on Fire) made with *cidra* (champagne) and *domé* (a Spanish cognac). In the morning he used to send me off to get his "coffee." He would sit back and enjoy several cups throughout the day. "Tell the man I want two coffees," he would say. Marcelino was sad when I told him that I would be leaving the shop. Around that time is when I met my teacher Jesús Pérez and started on the path to become a drummer.

DRUM LINEAGE: PABLO ROCHE AND JESÚS PÉREZ

Vamos a ver, vamos a ver, where to begin? Pablo Roche. He was the father of it all. *Akilakpa,* the principal teacher of all the students, followers, or apprentices of the batá. I learned from Jesús Pérez, *Oba Ilu* (King of the Town, or King of the Drum), who was a student of Pablo Roche's. They called Pablo Roche Akilakpa, which means "Hands of Gold" (*Manos de Oro*) in Yoruba.[13] He had Obatalá made; his name in ocha was Olufan Deyi. I met Jesús in 1955 and was his student for many years. He was my *padrino* when I made Changó, and I baptized one of his daughters (Lucía). He died by my side in 1985. What I know of the batá, I owe it all to Jesús Pérez. He was, is, and will always be my teacher, forever and ever. Amen.

Pablo Roche's father, Andrés Roche, learned to drum with Africans. They called him Andrés Sublime because he played so well. He taught Pablo, who lived in Guanabacoa, and he taught all those old drummers how to play, every last one of them, *todos.* There were *africanos de nación, criollos,* and *reyollos.* Andrés was criollo, which means he was born in Cuba but his parents were straight from Africa (*de nación*). Pablo was reyollo, a child of the criollos. His grandparents were Africans. Both Andrés and Pablo could play any instrument well. They had plenty of time; they could decide if they wanted to work and how hard. For a while, Pablo officially worked at the Instituto Cubano de Petroleo, where they refined gasoline, but he would have a guy stand in for him so he could do other things. He was a hustler (*pícaro*). He was no mechanic, carpenter, or anything like that. Pablo was a *garrotero,* which means he lent money with interest; he gave you a dollar and you paid him back a buck twenty-five! In his spare time Pablo made everybody's drums. He made drums for Nicolás Angarica, Moñito [José Valdés Frías], and that other guy, what's his name . . . El Ciego [Andrés Bacin, who was blind] because they had all learned and studied with him. Back in the day, there were no more than five fundamento drums in Havana. That's all. Pablo made all the fundamento drums except for the ones made by Adofó. The last set he made was for Jesús in 1954.

Pablo Roche spoke Lucumí because Miguel Ajayí taught him how. Miguel spoke Lucumí very well because his parents and grandparents had taught him. He spoke and sang Lucumí so well that even though he didn't have ocha made, they would always call him to sing *la llama* for initiation ceremonies, which he would do from outside the sacred room because he had no crown. Miguel spoke one dialect of Yoruba from a certain area, and Oba Di Meji (and therefore Angarica, whom he taught) spoke another way, a different dialect. Like the difference between Spanish from Havana and Santiago de Cuba: they say we sing when we speak, but they are the ones who sing, just like folks from the Dominican Republic. One day Nicolás Angarica said Pablo couldn't speak Lucumí. When Pablo heard this he got pissed and pulled a gun! Pablo was a tough guy (*guaposo*). The *mokongo* of *Munandibá* (leader of an important Abakuá lodge). He went around with a gun. Yes he did! He drove a four-door, black Cadillac and wore a hat made of pineapple leaves too. Jesús used to tell me, "Be happy!" because Pablo used to hit drummers who were grown men.

Once Pablo happened by a toque near his house in Guanabacoa. The drums playing belonged to a guy called Luis la Guajira. A priest possessed by Changó cornered Pablo and said he wanted to hear him play something special. Pablo responded that he would only play with his own drums, which he then went home and brought back to the party. As serious as a heart attack, Pablo told the guys playing the other drums

Pablo Roche, circa 1954. *Photo by Fernando Ortiz. Courtesy of Carlos Aldama.*

that if they sat down to play his drums, they could never play the others again. And that was it. All those drummers stayed with Pablo and the other drums were sunk.

Pablo ran off many of his older drummers at a certain point because he saw young people like Jesús and Nasakó, and he wanted to take advantage of it. Pablo, *cabrón* (rascal) that he was, said to himself, "I'm gonna knock everybody in Regla out the box with this crew of drummers." In the old days, becoming a drummer was very selective. The drummer was the kind of guy looking for a complement to his life, looking to fill some open space. For example, Jesús was a carpenter. He liked drumming but he didn't know anything about it, and by chance he met up with Pablo Roche. Jesús was going steady with and had a child by Pablo's next-door neighbor, La China. Pablo baptized their child and asked Jesús if he wanted to learn how to play batá. Pablo knew that Jesús was a carpenter and could easily learn to make drums, which was a needed skill. If you could make furniture you could make drums, right? At one point, Jesús, Trinidad Torregosa, Pedro Aspirina, and some others created a battery called *La Atómica* (the explosive one). Pablo put a stop to that when he showed up at one of their gigs with his revolver!

I never played with Pablo myself. He played when they presented my sister to the drum in Párraga (a neighborhood in Havana), but I was too young to see. They presented her twice, once in Matanzas because one of her godparents was from there and once in Havana. In Matanzas, Carlos Alfonso played the presentation along with Chachá. Carlos Alfonso was a *mulato* who used to play with a suit and tie. He gave Pablo Roche, Jesús Pérez (okónkolo), and Águedo Morales (itótele) the nickname of the Three Columns (Tres Columnas) because they were so strong. One day they played a Bajuba for Changó that was so fiery and sweet that Carlos stood up and shouted, "Stop playing right now! You guys are the Three Columns that never fall!" I didn't see it myself, but I know that Pablo and Carlos played together at some point.

[LISTEN TO TRACK 29]

I only saw Pablo Roche play once with my own eyes. It was in Guanabacoa in one of the main houses that always had toques. I had gone to an Abakuá *plante* (ceremony), then I stumbled on a *wemilere* and there was this incredible man playing. I said, "Damn that brother can play!" I was only about fifteen years old and I had no idea who he was. It wasn't until later that I talked to Jesús and learned that it was Pablo Roche. When Pablo would get up, then Pedro Aspirina would sit down, he was Pablo's

Standing, Fernando Ortiz; *Seated left to right,* Águedo Morales, Pablo Roche, and Jesús Pérez: The Three Columns, circa 1936. *Photo by Fernando Ortiz. Courtesy of Carlos Aldama.*

official segundero. At that point Pablo was already pretty old. When he died I'd say he was seventy-something. He still had his mind, but he was old, his body hurt. His wife Amelia, who had Ochun, would give him massages. On the same day the rebels assaulted the Presidential Palace going after Batista, Pablo Roche died. March 13, 1957. That same day. At the funeral Miguel Somodevilla played iyá, Macho played okónkolo, and Águedo Morales played itótele. Carlos Alfonso died making love shortly after Pablo.

I played the famous drum "Voz de Oro" (Golden Voice) after Pablo had died. I never actually played with him. Pablo was very close to Jesús. But even still I never got to develop that kind of relationship with him because he died soon after. I wasn't that into drumming yet anyway. I did get to play with Mario Aspirina, Nasakó, Macho, Andrés Isaaqui, and Oba Dola, the father of Papo Angarica. At that time I saw Jesús from time to time but it was very dangerous to go around Havana; there had been attacks on the Presidential Palace, because of the bombs, the revolutionary struggle. When Pablo died I learned of his funeral in Guanabacoa through my sister, but I didn't go. I went to Jesús's house and everyone was gone to the funeral.

Jesús wrote a book that he gave to Rogelio Martínez Furé, the researcher for Conjunto Folklórico Nacional, who gave it to the Ministry of Culture, but it's never been published.[14] Somebody must have it. Guillermo Barreto wrote out the toques, with the songs and everything.

There has to be something inside that draws you to the drums. It has to be your destiny. It's not just that you want to play. There are so many guys that I know who would love to be drummers, but they can't. It's not for them. I had one friend who thought he could be a drummer simply because he was a son of Changó. But no! It was not in him. I was about fifteen years old when I started playing with Jesús Pérez. He worked across the street from my house on Salud. My first drum lessons were in the street. It was for my own lack of respect (*por una falta de respeto mía*) that I became a drummer.

Jesús was a big, strong black man. *Muy bonito* (very handsome). He walked with style and had nice jewelry, *un negro lindo* (beautiful black man). He walked in the middle of the street like this [struttin']. I was just a teenager and I used to joke to myself, as big as this guy is walking like that he must be a sissy! He worked right across the street from my house in a *carpintería* (carpentry shop) called Martí. Plus he was a close friend of my father and mother. Jesús was Abakuá and so was my dad, so they would talk. During this time I worked as a tailor. So one day around lunchtime I came home to find Jesús – who knew I used to joke about him. I would laugh because he used to wear big, extravagant jewelry. He knew but he never said anything about it. Besides, I had never directly insulted him to his face or anything – I would just be cracking up from across the street, you know.

One day after my lunch I found him talking with my mom and dad at the door of our apartment in our *solar*.[15] My father asked Jesús if he knew me and Jesús answered "¡Sí, yo conozco el muchacho!" (Yes, I know him.) "What's the problem, *ecobio*?" my dad asked.[16] "Nothing, I just see him sitting across the street all the time." He wasn't going to tell my dad about the jokes, but he was letting me know! I thought I was going to be in trouble with my dad. I left and went back to work at the shop. Two or three days later I ran into Jesús. Remember he worked in the furniture factory across the street. Trinidad Torregosa and those other drummers, I knew them because they would always be around too. But Jesús lived in Cayo Hueso. So then he said to me *"Te voy a invitar a un lugar,* I'm going to invite you somewhere. And it's not far." Okay. He invited me to a tambor on Jesús Peregrino Street between Soledad and Castillero, right there in the barrio of Pueblo Nuevo, near his house. "I want you to see something there." When I got there, *coño,* and saw the drums . . . I had never seen batá drums before. *Bembé, güiro, rumba, comparsa,* yes, but not batá. Not because it was secret, just because I had not been around it (*no era mi ambiente*). And my sister had ocha made. But I don't remember going when they presented her to the drum. She is my madrina.

These drums sound great! *¡Coño, de pinga!* (Shit goddamn). I was so excited as I entered the tambor. After a while Jesús got up from the drum and invited me to a bar on the corner. *"Pon un 'and dos'"* He told the bartender – this meant a beer and two glasses – because in Cuba before the revolution when you ordered a glass of beer, they filled your glass and saved the rest of the bottle for the next customer. Pon un "and dos." I said, "The drums sound great!" "You like them?" he asked. "Yes, I am going to learn to play!" "Well, you're not going to learn shit from me (*ni pinga*)!" "Why not?" "Because I own the drums, and since you make all those jokes about me, even though I'm Abakuá from *Oru Apapá akondominamefe sese bibiokondorá chambeleke chambelekawa ekwe entemesoro,* that's why you won't learn!" "Hold on a minute, *espérate,* let's talk about this," I pleaded. But he wouldn't hear it. Jesús had me like this for about six months. I would go out to Guanabacoa or wherever. I knew he lived on Soledad or that I could find him at the carpintería, and I would track him down and ask again about the drums. He would shoo me away, "You are not going to learn a damn thing (*ni cojones*), so go away, go to work!"

One day I followed them to a toque in Guanabacoa for a man named Marqués, a white man, who lived in Cayo Hueso, and was an Abakuá from *Monandibá Efó,* like Jesús. He lived with an old santera called Omi Yomi from the barrio of Colón. He had money, and they went to play for him in Guanabacoa. The man had Obatalá made. When I arrived, Jesús asked, "What are you doing here?" I tried to explain again and he continued to say, "You are not going to play." At that, the old *tambolero* Amado

Gómez came up, and Jesús told him to sit me down to play okónkolo so I would stop pestering him (*pa' que no me joda más*). I had worn him down, tired him out. That was 1955. And I was always by his side after that (*no me despegué más nunca de él*).

When I was learning, Jesús never mistreated me. The most he would do was say I needed to play more and better or eat less at the ceremonial meal for drummers. I passed up Ricardo and a lot of other drummers in my studies. Soon after that, in 1957, Pablo died, then Carlos Alfonso. Later Amelia died. I was Jesús's favorite student. Like Jesús was for Pablo. Just the other day, if Jesús had been alive, he would have celebrated his ninetieth birthday. He was born on April 4, 1915, and died on April 5, 1985. I'm not the best drummer of all (*Yo no soy el mejor*). But I try my best to retain what I learned from Jesús, and *then* do my own thing. The problem is that some people want to create without having a base, and what it does is create confusion. You can't make a building without a foundation. Jesús taught me what Pablo had taught him. Now I am teaching you what Jesús taught me.

Jesús was the kind of man that everyone wanted to be around, *por su forma de ser*. He made tables, drawers, etcetera, and fixed Victrolas. He liked his drummers to be clean and to keep decent jobs. I came to wear jewelry because of him. You know why I wear this gold chain? Because of Jesús. "A drummer has to have something to adorn himself . . . *tienes que usar una cadena,* you need to have a chain." He had a humongous gold chain (*un cadenón grandísimo*) that he earned touring in Venezuela and Mexico. He would fiddle with one of his chains and say, "This is my favorite," suggesting all the time that I get one too. Finally I did. Jesús was like that. There were certain things he didn't like. One was that anybody around him would stink. He would say, "You didn't bathe today did you? I don't think you did!" He would even buy you a new shirt if you were broke (*jodido*); he would just give it to you. During that time the drummers used to wear PR, an English shirt that was sold in Cuba. "A drummer's got to be clean," Jesús would say. Once at a divination, Eleguá said I liked *cigaritos alegres* (marijuana) and Jesús said, "What!" Imagine if I tried to tell a youngster today that they shouldn't smoke, they wouldn't accept it.

Jesús Pérez drumming at the San Souci nightclub in Havana, circa 1952. *Courtesy of Carlos Aldama.*

Mira, chico, you can't give yourself popularity, people give it to you. Jesús was not the best drummer. I think he was popular because he would do anyone a favor. And he knew the business of drums. Understand? It came naturally to him. He had charisma. People would be stressing out, with all kinds of problems and they would say, "Let's go get Jesús." He would be in the shop, and he would agree to play and be paid whenever the person could manage. He helped people out. So folks kept coming back. He was pleasant; his character was good. Pablo wasn't like that; neither was Moñito. You would go to Moñito's house and he wouldn't even open the door, not even if he knew you. He would say "Talk to you later" and close the door right in your face. Trinidad was very handsome, but he was a bastard.[17] He was a son of Yemayá and was always throwing water around. They didn't have the same way with people Jesús had. People started going to Jesús because he liked to teach and you could learn quickly with him. Fermin had his own style, a lot of *banderas* to adorn his drums, and so on. Moñito was too mean (*insoportable*). Negrito was too busy doing *brujería.* He hardly played. For all these reasons people wanted to be part of Jesús's battery.

Trinidad was the one who worked closest with Fernando Ortiz. He gave the conferences and we would demonstrate with the drums. Trinidad owned a set of fundamento called Ako Bi Añá, which was for ceremonies. When they did the first demonstration in 1936, the santeros started talking about how Pablo was playing the drums in public in the theater *y qué sé yo qué sé cuando.* Pablo, who was wild, said, "You can all go to hell!" (*¡Vayan al carajo todos ustedes!*) But after that Pablo didn't play in public anymore, and that work went to Trinidad. He would call on Jesús, Armandito, and me to play. Sometimes at La Universidad de La Habana or in the Spanish part of Habana Vieja.

Nicolás Angarica had another important drum battery in Havana.[18] He was a godchild of Oba Di Meji, a famous diviner, who taught him directly. Nicolás worked more as an *obá* than as a drummer. So the responsibility for the drum fell on his sons, Papo and Sergio. Papo was into *guapería* (gangsterism); he was always around the comparsa group called La Jardinera. Then he got into trouble and had to slow down. Sergio worked on the docks, had a lot of jewelry; it was a trip. His hobby was cleaning shoes. Nicolás had Changó made. On October 15 every year he would

Trinidad Torregosa, circa 1954. *Photo by Fernando Ortiz. Courtesy of Carlos Aldama.*

have a toque for Oyá at his home, because his wife was initiated to that oricha. He was not a great drummer, God forgive me for saying it, but he was a heck of an obá, one of the best in Cuba. Because he was dedicated to making santos and divining, his real calling, he sent his crew off to play the drums. Mostly they played in the houses of his many godchildren, or in his own house. You understand? He was not a great drummer. Papo got his drums after he passed. Sergio made a fundamento from that one. Bolaños, Papaíto, Nené, Regino were all students of Nicolás Angarica. Nicolás was an obá, *asere*,[19] not a drummer.

The oldest players were always the official instrumentalists of each battery. The oldest players did the *oro seco*. In the case of Jesús's drum it was Andrés, Amado "*Jorobao*" (hunchback), sometimes with Ramiro, or other times with what's-his-name . . . the older drummers anyway. Then younger players might play the *oro cantado*. The strongest players would play again when it was time to really call the oricha, and make money. To finish the toques it was the older, established players who did it. They would close the *tambor* and play for eggun. Each set of drummers would have its time to play during the ceremony. I was the segundero for Jesús, and Ricardo played okónkolo. I wasn't a great okónkolo player. I learned it quick and let it go; I would play a little bit and get up, *no estoy pa' esto* (I've had enough). But I got very accustomed to playing itótele for Jesús. When Jesús got up I would leave itótele and sit down on iyá.

I played all the drums that existed in Havana during that era: Pablo's, Fermin's, Moñito's, Nicolas's, Adofó's, Trinidad's, and Jesús's drums. There weren't many drums and there weren't that many omo Añá either. When they decided they were going to let you play, they would ask Añá if it was okay. With that authorization, they would wash your hands. After that, they would just decide one day to swear you to the drum. In my case, I showed up at Trinidad's house one day and they had made the preparations for the ceremony. They said, "Change your clothes!" and it was on.

Back in the day, the *derecho* belonged to the owner of the drums. It would be seven or eight pesos, which at that time was good money. After that, the money that the santeros put in the jícara as they saluted the drums, plus the money that the oricha collected from people. Folks didn't put money on the throne. The oricha would go around and get money from people. This money was divided "por pilita" (nickels and dimes): some for the mayorcero, less for the segundero, the okonkolero, and so on. As an apprentice you could play all day and make pennies, almost nothing at all.

We would always place a gourd (*jícara*) right in front of the drums where santeros put money offerings to Añá for honoring their oricha.

We would throw toasted corn into the *jícara* in honor of Eleguá, to bring money. Jesús created the system of putting all the money in the jícara and dividing it half and half between the official singer and the drummers. Other singers or players could come, and if they sang well they earned money as they saluted santeros, and/or when the party was done, the owner of the drum might give them a little something too.

There used to be a ritual meal served to the drummers before any *toque*. The meal itself depended on the financial means of the hosts and how much they liked you. But generally they would ask the boss of the drummers what he wanted to eat, then go to the market at *cuatro caminos* and get it. In those days there was abundance. Plus, people loved Jesús because he would help them out. He would play for free and say, "I hope you smile like this when you bring me my money!" (*Quiero verte con la misma sonrisa.*) So we ate well. Red wine, *refresco,* and bread were obligatory. Beyond that it could be any kind of food. But it was the best of the best. Because from the oldest generation of drummers until Jesús's time, there was a great respect for drummers and we would be treated very well.

The table would be attended by a *santera* of any oricha except Changó. They are considered daughters of the king of the drums, so they can't be servants in this situation. The musicians would be served in order of seniority. Once everyone got his food, then we would begin to eat. We would wait for Jesús or the oldest, most respected drummer present to finish and dismiss the ceremony before getting up from the table. But today, especially here in California, all this has changed. There is confusion about the songs at the Añá table for hand washing and clearing the plates. Somehow songs from Ifá like *Ochimini eh awachama ikoko* made their way to the Añá table. The true Añá songs were sung only for special Añá ceremonies.

AÑÁ AT WORK

The presentation of iyawoses is an honor for drum batteries. It's a chance for the drums to complete their full range of functions: 1) Saluting the oricha in the altar room, 2) saluting the santeros outside during the *oro cantado,* 3) announcing and confirming new initiates to the community, and 4) calling down oricha to dance, give advice, and heal people at the party.

There are three ways to present iyawoses. First, drummers are presented like regular santeros. Drummers have a certain way to get presented – both when they have oricha crowned and when they don't. All presentations are done with the aim of announcing a new initiate to the community, whether drummer or priest – from Olodumare on down to the santeros and *aleyos* (non-initiates) too. Take for instance a drummer who does not have ocha made but has been sworn to the drum, you have to let the community know, Olodumare, that there is someone new. In another case a drummer who is already omo Añá may be making ocha. As part of his presentation as a santero you have to acknowledge that he is omo Añá by singing *Awade o ee* at the end. You present in a different way.

Regular santeros get presented dressed up with their *traje* (ceremonial outfit) and barefoot, or all in white with shoes. Matanzas style, they present by first singing to Eleguá while the iyawó is seated, then they go out with *Mariwo Ye* for Ogun. These are the different ways it's done. You can go around in the circle and back and forth as many times as you want. If the chorus is sweet and people are singing I may continue for a while. If not, it's quick . . . *pa'l piso,* to the floor to salute. The *oyugbona* (secondary initiating priest) accompanies the iyawó in the procession while the madrina or padrino (main initiator) waits for them near the drum. The other people around the iyawó are initiates who accompany them, just as other initiates accompanied them at some time. It's the continuity of time and life. The iyawó carries two coconuts and two candles on a plate and a *derecho* (money for Añá).[20] Back in the day it used to be just one *peso* or maybe a peso-and-a-half, depending on the oricha. Eleguá gets two coconuts, two candles, a cock, and a bottle of *aguardiente* (strong alcohol). Changó gets all that plus a bunch of green bananas or plantains. Some people release doves before a new initiate to Ochosi is made, as the person is brought into the house from the market. In the old days you would fire a shot. When this would be done in some far out neighborhood. But now the new initiate makes as if they are shooting a bow and arrow. After that, they enter in the room and their ceremony begins.

The plate gets put on the ground. And the iyawó's head goes on top of the coconuts. The padrino holds the iyawó's head and everyone including the drum prays. In Havana you lie down on the ground to do this. I present Havana style. Then the iyawó is brought up and dances for his or her *ángel de la guarda* (guardian angel, main oricha). Then the iyawó salutes Añá once more – first by laying out on the floor, then by placing their forehead on top of the iyá, then okónkolo, then itótele. After this, parents (if they are present), and then godparents are saluted. Then you are whisked out. In Matanzas they play Alaro Yemayá. Some in Havana do that too, but not me. I don't do it with music. Unless it's a drummer's presentation (not a santero), then after he's played all three drums we would sing *Awadeo e ilu awada,* and he would go back to the room.[21] I never really went to many presentations in Matanzas. Here in the U.S. people sometimes play Añá on the *día del medio,* and I don't agree with this. I present iyawoses after seven days, after the *itá.* It's only after itá that your life as a santero truly begins.

To be a ritual drummer you don't necessarily have to have ocha made. But there was a kind of continuity where through the drum you would end up making santo. In the first place you have an oricha, Añá, constantly on your lap. Two, when you play for a presentation of an iyawó, you are receiving someone that has been crowned with oricha. No matter how sworn you are to the drum, or how well your hands have been washed for Añá, still *la corona es la corona* (the crown is the crown) . . . you understand? If I don't have ocha made, then logically I cannot present *iyawoses.* Back in the day, only drummers who were santeros could play presentations. Why? Because they had been crowned, so they could welcome newly crowned initiates. Drummers would play the *oro,* the *cantado,* then when it was time to play the *presentación,* all those who did not have ocha would have to get up, and drummers with ocha would sit down to play. It's *La Regla de Ocha:* I have to have received something in order to pass it on to you. That's how it was. They let Andrés Isaaqui play to present iyawoses only because he was such an old *tambolero,* from Pablo Roche's time, that's the only reason. Amado had Obatalá. Armando Sotolongo had Eleguá. Giraldo had Changó, Lázaro Obatalá, El Chino had Obatalá, Bolaños had Eleguá, Regino Yemayá. Now no. Drummers without ocha play presentations.

In the past, they used to present new initiates twice, once in Havana and once in Matanzas, so that Añá from both places would recognize them. It's been lost now. But they did this with my sister, who is my madrina. The intensity level for presenting an *iyawó* to the drum is not the same as when you're playing *oro seco*. It's higher, *más fuerte*. Godparents like to see their *ahijados* mounted. Trinidad Torregosa was the one who sang when I was presented. Drummers, by the way, shouldn't get mounted, especially not while playing. But if one day Changó were to come to my head, I couldn't tell him no! It happened to Fantoma, a big time Abakuá and drummer, who got possessed while playing iyá. They stopped the drum, took him into the *igbodú* and kept on rolling. What else could they do?

ETIQUETTE

There were religious houses in Cuba where you couldn't hit on any women at the party. Or where there was no alcohol served. These were rules that the drummers would follow, that shifted from house to house. Jesús didn't play around with this stuff either. For example, one time one of his drummers got really drunk at a toque, so Jesús suspended him. He told the guy he couldn't play for a while and not to come to any toques until Jesús told him it was okay. I don't know why, but the guy showed up at a toque and started playing. When Jesús arrived and saw him there, he got pissed and took the drum away. Jesús never let that guy play with our battery again. This would have hurt the prestige of the group.

The day before a drummer plays fundamento drums, ones that have Añá, he should sleep clean (*dormir limpio*). When a drummer says "*Estoy sucio*" (I'm dirty), he means that the night before he made love. *Mira lo que te voy a decir,* listen to this. There was a lady named Migí. She had Obatalá made and she kept the dates of the toques we would play with Jesús. Everybody would go to her to make sure when and where different toques would happen. But one day Migí – who always ran numbers and cooked for the neighborhood hookers – she forgot that Jesús had a tambor to do. Who knows why, but she forgot. And there I am sitting in front of the carpintería – because Jesús lived upstairs and the shop where he fixed Victrola jukeboxes was downstairs. Jesús lived at Soledad 415 between San Rafael and San Miguel Streets and I lived at Zanja 668 entre

Soledad y Aramburo. So all I had to do was go up the street and around the corner to get to his house.

So we were there one day shooting the breeze (*comiendo mierda*) and here come the folks who were giving the tambor. "Jesús, *¿qué pasa, compadre?* Our house is full of santeros waiting for you to play!" So they called Migí and, sure enough, she had forgotten all about it. Jesús kept calm, "No problem, we can still play." And at that I leaned over and let him know I was *sucio* (dirty). "What?" he spit back, and I explained how I was living with my woman and I even had children, you know, nature. He told me to find Ricardito and a few other drummers to play the tambor. He told me a few things to do, a cleaning, *pin pan,* he said to play *suavecito,* not too hard and that was it.

When we got back from the tambor I was ready to head home. But Jesús said, "No don't go just yet, strip and get in the bath tub." "What in the hell!?" I thought. "I'll bathe at home, are you crazy!?" He told me again more forcefully to get in the tub. *Está bien,* I did what he said, but I didn't want him thinking I was a sissy or anything [laughter], if it had been anyone else telling me to do this I would have said "What the fuck is wrong with you!?" So he gave me hot water and told me "Scrub yourself with this plant (*hierba*), because today you played." Okay, I drenched myself with the water and heard him call "Scrub hard!" I grabbed some of the plant and went like this [scrubbing] and it was *quitamaldición,* which has small thorns underneath the leaves. I hollered as I scratched myself all over "¡¡¡Ayy!!!" Jesús hollered back, "That's so you never forget that you have to be clean to play!" I had what looked like claw marks all over my body for about fifteen or twenty days. "But Jesús I told you!" "I know, but this way you will never forget: *Cuando uno hace el amor al otro día no toca.*"

Jesús always played beautifully, *siempre.* There were two toques he loved to play: *Alaro de Yemayá* and *Meta* for Changó. He played everything *muy bonito.* Jesús had his own personality, and over the years I copied it. The only thing I couldn't get was his soul! That very personal creativity he had, and that Pablo also had. I didn't take his soul, so to speak, because I couldn't, it was his. I did emulate him though, and after a while I had his style down pat. Sometimes as I would play he'd say "Hey, that's mine!" "Yeah, but I like it." "Don't forget it's mine!" he would say, laughing. But in Alaro Yemayá, Meta Changó, and Bajuba Changó it was like, Damn! He played so sweet. No one could play like him, *nadie*. People would say Pablo, Jesús, and then they would say Carlos. "Who is playing? Is it Pablo, Carlos, or Jesús?" And it was me. Way back in the day when drummers played you could tell who they were. You created your own personality.

[LISTEN TO TRACKS 26 AND 29]

Jesús used to say, "I messed up, right?" And I would say "No," knowing he had really messed up. That was my respect for him. For me *el maestro* never makes a mistake. But I knew he did. I was his segundero for about fifteen years. He was a very . . . creative person. Creative, but *en la medida* (on beat, in swing). He would play an adornment and it might not fit quite right and he would say, "Keep going!" as he worked it out. I would say to myself, "Here he goes inventing again." He was looking to fit his new thing into the flow of the rhythm. He might mess up, then he would go back and play it again. After all those years of playing with Jesús, people asked who was playing, him or me. On itótele I could read his mind. I knew all his tricks. He would ask me about mistakes he felt he had made. But to me the teacher never makes a mistake. I have that respect.

You have to create your own personality. Back in the day you would know who was playing without seeing. We recognized each other. Each drummer had his virtues, his own qualities and characteristics. For example, Armando el Sordo, was very strong, sublime, religious. He spoke dialect like the Africans. He was Abakuá. He played the clarinet *and* he was deaf. He would always break Jesús's drums, he would play so hard. To the point where Jesús put a thick-ass goatskin on the drum and dared him "Break that!"

SINGERS

Josefina (La Chiquitica), José Antonio el Cojo, and Maximiliano (Baba Sikú) were the great singers in Havana during my era. People would get excited if they knew José Antonio was going to sing. After Josefina Aguirre, in order of age and seniority as singers, came El Bravo, then Amelia Pedroso, José Antonio, Pedrito, El Ñato, and the other one who sang only for *eggun* (the ancestors) . . . Baba Sikú was his name. These were the crème-of-the-crop singers of that time, the 1950s. Remember that back then there were singers for oricha on one hand, and singers for eggun on the other. Baba Sikú (who had Changó made) was Jesús Pérez's padrino. He was not interested in singing for ocha, only for eggun. Some stupid people say they never go to eggun toques, because they're afraid. But eggun [toques] are the cleanest toques there are, that's where you cleanse yourself. It's at oricha parties where you pick up other people's negative energy. Think about it, no one gives a tambor just because they want to. It's always for some problem to be solved, some debt to an oricha, something. So this *arayé*, this *ossogbo* is being picked up by everybody. The *tambor de eggun* is where you clean yourself.

José Antonio, Pedrito . . . they were sharp (*pícaros*). They were the next generation of great singers. All of them learned from Josefina Aguirre, or Josefina Caballito. The singer Lázaro Ros used to work at a chicken place cleaning chickens. Trinidad Torregosa introduced him to important folks, and Jesús put him to work as a singer. This was in the late 1950s. There was Pedrito Saavedra, Amelia Pedroso; Merceditas was never really an ocha singer. Trinidad taught her, she lived around the corner from him. We worked with her on TV and the radio. She was a cabaret singer and a priestess of Ochun. On her ocha birthdays she would invite six people and buy six of everything (for example), and as soon as people had eaten those things, it was "*¡Fuera!*" (Get out!).

DRUMMERS

The drummer who learned the most from Pablo was Raúl Díaz Nasakó. He was Pablo's favorite student along with Jesús. He and Jesús were about the same age. He was around Pablo 24–7. He didn't do anything else. While Jesús went to work at the carpentry shop, Nasakó was conversing with Pablo. He liked the *gando* (*prenda*/witchcraft) too. Nasakó was always at a *Palo* ceremony, and in fact, he got his name for always

Standing, Pablo Roche and Pablo Rodríguez; *seated,* Trinidad
Torregosa, Raúl "Nasakó" Díaz, Giraldo Rodríguez, circa 1954.
Photo by Fernando Ortiz. Courtesy of Carlos Aldama.

doing brujería. When he didn't have anything else to do he would go to
Pablo's house. They would talk Abakuá, because Nasakó was the *empeó*
(judge) of a lodge called *Feabakuá* and Pablo the *mokongo* of *Oru Apapá.*

But Nasakó was not a very strong player. He knew a lot. But when it
came time to play. He was kind of a pretty boy (*siempre estaba de figurín*).
He didn't like to bust up his hands. He was handsome, very respectful,
and people respected him. But he didn't give himself to the drum one
hundred percent. *Mira,* he didn't make or fix drums. He didn't know how
to put on skins, lace, or carve – remember during that era there were no
lathes (*torno*). You had to get a piece of tree trunk, make a hole (*meterle
gubia*) and burn that out with coal (*carbón*). Then you would knock and
pick out the burnt wood from inside. After you made the hole through
the center of the drum, you would then focus on the hourglass shape
outside. Nasakó didn't do these things.

Miguel Somodevilla was a very conservative older man (*señor*).
Very quiet, it was hard to get a word out of him. If you would ask him

a question he wouldn't answer, he would just look at you and play with the chaworó on the drum. After he got used to you and saw you were a respectful youngster he would warm up. Mario Aspirina worked on the docks. Inocente was a *chapista* (auto body repairman). He was always in jail. Pedrito worked in the *matalero* (as a butcher).

Bolaños, for example, never sweated when he played. He would wear a nice button-up shirt and play without ever sweating. Trinidad Torregosa was also called Mayito Menocal; he was chauffer for the president of Cuba until he had an accident that stopped him. He was president of the well-respected Afro-Cuban society called Club Magnetti. But he wasn't the type of drummer to beat up his hands playing; he would play a while, and then his arm would cramp and he would get up, saying "I'm done, help me straighten out my arm!"

Andrés Isaaqui who played his chachá with just his two fingers had his own style. Anastasio was strong (*fuerte*). In Papo's case, he was into comparsa, and the life, until he got shot and got into *Ifá*. Jesús got popular along with Trinidad working in cabarets like the San Souci. He had more *ambiente de fiesta* (a festive vibe). He had gold chains, women, it was a whole other thing. Plus his drum played every day. Bolaños, Papaíto, Regino, all those folks started going to play for Jesús. Justasio, Amadito, Andrés. They called Jesús Benny Moré, women fighting over him *y todo eso*.

I don't really know who Pancho Quinto played with, *chico*. Pancho Quinto wasn't a batá drummer. He was more of a rumbero. Pancho was a *quinto* player who used *cajones* (boxes), a dockworker. He could turn out a rumba party by playing on just a chair! We played together in the *comparsa* procession Los Dandy de Belén. One day I saw him playing batá, and that was it. He always played well and still does – I hope he's living because he had been sick[22] ... that's my good friend, no my brother – but what happened? He had gone to learn from Jesús. And Jesús ... *ya tú sabes* [makes motor sounds, as if to say Jesús taught Pancho a lot so that he could take off as a batalero]. Later on he got a set of *fundamento* as well, but they weren't from Jesús.

I was always a serious drummer. Not so much into hanging out, and such. In the old days it was stricter (*había más rectitud*). With the old *santeros* and *santeras*, if you didn't play well for them they wouldn't even put their head on the drum to salute, they would turn their backs and leave. This was an embarrassment to your teacher. It meant they hadn't taught you well. There was a harder concept. Today we are in another generation. I can be hard on my son, but on other youngsters I can't do that, it won't work. Because they weren't born during my times, understand? There is more flexibility today. Among drummers you used to find all types – pot-heads, drunkards . . . everything except for homosexuals. Back in the day musicians were not gay. The musician was generally *mujeriego* (a womanizer) who liked *la mala noche* (serious partying). It was hard to find a gay musician. If you did, he was usually the piano player. "He's a pianist" became a way to call someone gay as a joke.

Thanks to the gays . . . free-living people (*gente de libre vivir*), the religion (Santería) has spread like wild fire. Leave it up to men [heterosexuals] and there would hardly be any toques. A guy will only give a toque as a last resort. If he can get away with it, he'll give Changó two roosters and two candles and that's it, *pa' la pinga albañiles que se acabó la mezcla* (to hell with it). But *el pato*, he gives a tambor *porque le gusta* . . . because he loves that feeling, it's the only place in the world where he can enjoy a certain prestige, surrounded by so many godchildren. He might be gay but he has a hundred and fifty ahijados! She's a *tortillera* but has fifty ahijadas! It's gays that have really opened the road and the world for the religion . . . people like Ocha Güeye, Nicolás Hernández.

I did a hell of a lot to learn the drum (*Me jodí mucho con cojones*). Sometimes I would play all day at a toque and they would pay me two pesetas. I carried drums, cleaned skins, and toted coconuts. I paid with my dedication. I didn't go to parties and things because I'd be at toques. They used to call me *el coquero* (the coconut man) because I had to carry all the coconuts that santeros gave to the drum when we played. People would tease me and laugh. People would say I was gonna burn out my brains from practicing so much. My dad said all those big guys would break me in two. But I didn't care. It was my destiny to become a drummer.

3

Batá in the Revolution

* Umi *

In 1959, Cuba began to reinvent itself under the direction of Fidel Castro's revolutionary socialist government. Historically in Cuba, poor people – especially Afro-Cubans – were marginalized. Now after centuries of colonial and neocolonial rule, poor people and blacks gained access to the delights of the nation. The debate has raged since Cuba's first independence struggle (from 1868 to 1878) about whether blacks are mere beneficiaries of white benevolence who should be thankful for their freedom, independence, education, opportunities, and so on, or co-authors/owners of all of Cuba's revolutionary history – as soldiers, thinkers, and perhaps the truest carriers of the spirit of freedom in Cuba. Carlos's grandfather was a *mambí* (rebel soldier in the Cuban War of Independence, 1895 to 1898) and his father was a founding member of the Cuban State Security after the revolution of 1959. Despite some improvement in conditions for black Cubans, the denigration and repression of Afro-Cuban religions has persisted even under the new Castro regime. The revolution has passed through several moments, each with its own consequences for Santería and batá.

During the earliest revolutionary period at the beginning of the 1960s, religion was largely left alone. Afro-Cuban folkloric music was actually promoted (including batá and other drumming styles with ties to religion). This was the period that saw the creation of the Conjunto Folklórico Nacional, of which Carlos was a founding member. The increasing tension between Cuba and the United States that culminated in

65

the Bay of Pigs invasion (which Carlos describes from his perspective), as well as ideological shifts within the revolutionary leadership, altered the regime's position on religion. Religious groups were suspected of harboring anti-revolutionary agitators or cultivating worldviews and behaviors among the people that were incompatible with the new revolutionary culture. Conflicts with Christians surfaced quickly, in part because of the close ties between Catholicism and the social elite. This group was seen as a direct political threat. Tensions with Afro-Cuban groups surfaced somewhat later, stemming from long-standing prejudices in middle-class Cuban society against African-derived culture and aggravated by Marxist philosophy.[1] The revolutionary government considered Afro-Cuban religions to be obstacles to constructing a modern, technically oriented socialist society. They were remnants from the past that had to be removed. Although all Cuban governments from the nineteenth century on have consistently suppressed Afro-Cuban religious practices, the most organized and articulated policy of repression came from the early revolutionary government itself.[2]

As of the mid-1960s, officials required celebrants to apply for a permit in order to hold a *toque de santo,* as had been the case during the pre-revolutionary period. Applications involved submitting forms thirty days in advance with lists of all participants, information on how much money would be charged by the drummers, a photo of the person, if any, "making their saint," and an explanation of why they wanted to do so.[3] Carlos mentions how the state confiscated the animals that he had bought for use in his Santería initiation ceremony in 1971. Singer Merceditas Valdés, who worked closely with Ortiz performing alongside Jesús Pérez and Carlos Aldama in the 1950s, and who had built her career performing the music of Santería, found herself unable to perform this repertoire publicly for decades because authorities maintained strict limits on the quantity of religious music on the radio and television. In the book *Afro-Cuban Voices,* a batá drummer named Juan Benkomo from Havana recalls that "If you were religious, you couldn't be in the [Communist] party . . . [and] to be singled out as religious was to be socially ostracized."[4] Batá drummer Felipe García Villamil refused to join the party because he knew that his religious practices were contrary to revolutionary doctrine.[5] The hostility Carlos sees in fellow practitioners' eyes when he unwittingly enters a ceremony with his government-issue military uniform on reflects the tension between the religious communities and the revolutionary authorities.

In Cuba, arts like batá drumming are studied, preserved, shaped, and promoted as what is called *cultura* (culture), which entails government controls, commercialization, and the reframing of Afro-Cuban religion as entertainment and/or the object of academic study rather than as living spiritual practice.[6] Groups like the Conjunto Folklórico Nacional de Cuba, Los Muñequitos de Matanzas, Grupo Afro Cuba de Matanzas, and others were supported or created to valorize elements of traditional culture while simultaneously pursuing ideological initiatives. They aimed to "elevate" folk expression, professionalize it, and make it more intelligible to urban, and indeed international, audiences.[7] These troupes and their events are organized and coordinated within an impressive state mechanism.

The folkloric companies coexist with communities of actual believers. Within those communities, people variously appreciate, detest, or even study the stage versions of the tradition. Many feel that the folklorization of Afro-Cuban sacred traditions is a way to rescue them from disrepute and to honor them with a dignified place in Cuban society. Others decry folklorization as a strategy to undermine and destroy the Afro-Cuban religions, thereby eliminating them as bases for resistance against ongoing systems of racial inequality. For instance, musicologist Helio Orovio considered the Conjunto Folkórico Nacional de Cuba to be a "cultural reservation" intended by the government to be the only outlet for many forms of Afro-Cuban expression that it ultimately did not want to see perpetuated.[8] Considering that both perspectives hold validity, this created an ironic situation in which the socialist government at once promoted and endangered Santería, batá, and so on. The dancers and singers from the Conjunto labor to recreate a bit of the magic that happens in a "real" *fiesta de santo,* but without the religious belief system and history that would typically inform it.[9] Carlos feels aspects of this tension when practitioners challenge him about the appropriateness of his work with the Conjunto. He defends himself emphatically: "I have never brought the religion to the stage. What I have done is to take *elements from the religion* for use in the theater. The difference is in my behavior, my state of mind, my intention." Whether the presentation of staged folkloric performances helps or hurts the Santería and batá traditions remains an open question.

Carlos's discussion of the Conjunto Folklórico Nacional brings out conflicts between Cuba's revolutionary leadership (primarily white) and the rank-and-file members of the group (black). It is ironic that the revolutionary government created and funded the Conjunto, providing opportunities for black musicians like Carlos to travel the world, raise families, have homes, and so on, and still Carlos calls them racist and offers occasions when this was exemplified by negative attitudes and comments by the leadership. He focuses especially on the treatment of "informant-performers," those founding members of the group who were steeped in the actual Afro-Cuban religious traditions that were being reinterpreted for stage presentation.[10] To him, their replacement by trained dancers seems to reinscribe the historical disrespect from government and mainstream society toward Cuba's African roots. This echoes what I saw myself regarding common understandings and negative valuations of blackness in Cuba.[11] Racism exists in Cuba alongside the philosophy of Cuba Libre, and in spite of heroic efforts to erase its historical legacy.

Carlos respectfully criticizes artists like Lázaro Ros and Merceditas Valdés as having prioritized the stage over participating in actual religious ceremonies. (In the case of Ros, Carlos may be too harsh, as Ros is revered by many precisely as a ritual singer.)[12] Carlos underlines the fact that throughout his career as a performer in the Conjunto, Grupo Oru, and others, he was also constantly involved in making music at ceremonies. His thrilling description of the Yemayá procession in Regla ironically reveals details from a world of Santería and batá practice that began to disappear at least partly due to the efforts of the revolutionary government for which he worked.

In professionalizing and staging Afro-Cuban folklore, musicians like Carlos became government workers rather than (or in addition to) artisan entrepreneurs within the Santería community. The result was that some Afro-Cubans from humble origins, like the founding members of the Conjunto, were able to travel the world and make lives for themselves that would have been impossible without the revolution and its projects in *cultura*. At the same time, this situation created a separation and a new kind of dialogue between real communities of practitioners on one hand and the choreographers, scholars, and administrators that studied them as the "raw material" from which to create theatrical art on the other. Sometimes what real santeros did within their fiestas came from what they had seen on stage. Carlos offers the example of a well-known Santería song that is commonly sung to invoke Yemayá the oricha of the sea, but which is really for another oricha, Ochosi, the hunter. According to Carlos, in this case a change made within a Yemayá piece that the Conjunto put together affected practice within the oricha houses.

In another trajectory of dialogue between the religious community, the stage, and the world "out there," what outsiders learned about Santería and batá came increasingly from members of the folklore companies. They were the ones being exposed to international audiences in Cuba and abroad. These interactions were related to communities of real santeros, because many company members were *religiosos* too; but now cultural information was being bartered and prestige reckoned outside of the previously established frameworks of apprenticeship and ritual practice. Musicians and dancers who may have been highly respected within their ritual communities (after all, this is partly why they were chosen for the Conjunto) could be classified as mediocre performers and dismissed after sharing their knowledge (their *fundamento*) with the troupe. There is a shift from authority and status generated by lineage, competition, and patronage in the neighborhood to one constituted through centralized folkloric production in the Conjunto. Resentment and allegations by troupe members of racism on the part of the Conjunto leadership led to actual violence within the group, which Carlos describes. His reflections suggest a few questions: Does the racism or anti-racism of the Conjunto model reside principally in the individual negative attitudes of white academics? Or is racism more deeply embedded in the project of folklore itself (and its institutional structures), even when the individuals involved long for it to succeed as an anti-racist project?

Meanwhile, beyond the Conjunto, the nearly universal socialization of the Cuban economy facilitated the entry of Afro-Cubans into universities and occupations that had been previously closed to them.[13] The emigration of large sectors of the middle and upper classes in the aftermath of the revolution eased this process as well. As a result, religious practice *en el barrio* (in the neighborhood) changed. For example, the Yemayá procession in Regla came to an end and many practitioners renounced their oricha for careers inside of the revolutionary government. Carlos calls these people "brainwashed" and notes that some of them fell ill, went crazy, or even died after abandoning their family traditions. However, he also encourages his teacher's son Kimani to pursue a career as a surgeon *instead* of becoming a drummer and continuing the tradition of his father. This signals that Carlos too saw some value in the new opportunities created through the revolution. It also speaks to Carlos's dissatisfaction with the drum community during this period in his life. It reminds us as well of how relatively new the batá tradition was in Cuba. Jesús Pérez did not learn from his father, as he would have as a member of an Añá lineage in Yorubaland, but rather from a patriarch mentor. In fact Jesús's father was not a drummer. Reckoned this way, Kimani's decision was no real rupture of tradition at all. The disappearance of Carlos Aldama's world quite practically relates to opportunities provided by the revolution to be party bosses or doctors with sanction from broader society instead of spiritual leaders or artisans in the community.

  Carmelo Mesa-Lago, in his study *The Economy of Socialist Cuba,* acknowledges that the revolution significantly reduced race inequalities in income, education, health, social security, and, to a lesser extent, housing. He suggests also, however, that after two decades of revolution, significant racial inequalities persisted. Afro-Cubans were overrepresented in all diseases, especially those associated with poverty. Blacks were underrepresented in the best-paid, most prestigious, and highly skilled occupations and overrepresented in the worst paid, least prestigious, low-skilled occupations, hence income differences were still noticeable. Also, the majority of Afro-Cubans continued to live in the same housing they occupied at the beginning of the revolution because, even though they had the worst housing in 1958, moves into new housing or that left by exiles represented only one-fifth of total housing stock. Long after the revolution was underway, blacks had improved somewhat their housing standards, but still inhabited the worst of the existing stock.[14] During the 1970s and 1980s, the Cuban government harassed religious practitioners as part of an increased effort to enforce "scientific atheism" in Cuba. Atheist revolutionaries maintained a negative stance toward Afro-Cuban religions, which was a continuation of pre-revolutionary attitudes.[15] So, in addition to the new presence on the concert stage and greater educational and employment opportunities for black Cubans, Santería and batá continued to live underground at the margins of Cuban society.

Starting in the mid-1970s, intolerant attitudes toward religion and related music began to soften gradually. The social justice work by the Catholic Church and by Liberation Theology in other Latin American countries played a big role. Cuba's military involvement in Africa – in Algeria, Congo, Angola, and Ethiopia – had an effect too. By the end of the 1970s, more than three hundred thousand Cubans had been active combatants in Africa, and returned with a new appreciation for cultural forms that had long been stigmatized in Cuba.[16] The 1980s and 1990s witnessed a growing appreciation for Afro-Cuban arts once again. The state renewed efforts to document drum traditions and created additional performance spaces for them. Folkloric musicians like Carlos Aldama found ways to promote their heritage locally and internationally and earn a living as performers and teachers.[17]

The collapse of the Cuban economy at the start of the 1990s and the resulting crisis known as the "special period" affected all aspects of Cuban life, including Santería and batá. Whereas the tourism industry of the 1970s and 1980s was minimal, by the early 1990s tourism emerged as a strategy for economic survival. Many social ills such as prostitution, theft, drugs, and racism, which had receded with the efforts of the socialist government, reappeared and spread in the new economic situation. Blacks struggled to keep afloat in the mixed capitalist/socialist system that the government improvised in order to save the economy. The result has been a fundamental crisis of values.[18] The shady dealings among drummers that Carlos describes (stealing foreign students, etc.) reflect the desperation of the times for all Cubans, but especially Afro-Cubans, who had always been closer to the margins of society.

Carlos's emotional telling of how things seemed to fall apart after the death of his teacher Jesús Pérez calls attention to Cuba's crisis during the special period. Afro-Cubans feel the brunt of the shifts, as they have limited access to new opportunities created by changes in the Cuban economy. For example, Afro-Cubans receive few cash remittances from relatives abroad because most Cubans in diaspora are white, especially those with relative wealth in places like Miami. Also, Afro-Cubans are largely excluded from employment in new business ventures started in hopes of growing the economy by fomenting tourism. The deepest Santería practitioners and especially ritual drummers are black Cubans who occupy the lower levels of society in terms of economics and education. These details augment the context for Carlos's description of drummers scrambling for foreign students, fighting over drums, glory, and opportunity during Cuba's special period, which continues, to a large degree, up to the time of this writing. It is during this time too that Carlos notes an increase in "guapería" or violence around batá drum batteries. He goes as far as to compare the atmosphere of some batá ensembles to the unruly crowds at public dances held at places like La Tropical and El Polar.

After Jesús's death, Carlos lost out in the struggle over who would inherit his (Jesús's) *fundamento* drums. Hurt by this, Carlos faded almost totally out of the batá scene in Havana. Carlos feels that the respect accorded to batá drummers in general and to him personally eroded. Whereas drummers used to be served the best food at special meals before ceremonies, now they were served *picadillo de soya* – soy hash, which was a very common but not well-liked food during the special period. Rival drummers undercharged potential students or even claimed that Carlos was out of town or dead in order to keep students for themselves. At this point Carlos could really see the "golden age" receding. There is a shift here from traditional competition between drummers in the context of oricha houses and Santería, to competition among drummers on the open market seeking to capitalize on the new musical and spiritual tourism. The world Carlos had known and describes in chapter 2 seemed to be coming undone. These circumstances help to explain why Carlos would push his teacher Jesús's son to become a doctor rather than preserving (or really establishing) a family lineage as a drummer.

Much of Carlos's reflection on the dissolution of the tradition is narrated through the erosion of respect for him as a drummer and his marginalization from the social networks that provided *bataleros* with opportunities to play and earn a living. Once again we return to the question, Is the end of the golden age a personal or a community story?

* Carlos *

CONJUNTO FOLKLÓRICO NACIONAL DE CUBA

As far as Conjunto Folklórico goes, it all started in 1959 with a piece called Cantos y Leyendas Yorubas (Yoruba Songs and Legends), Yímbula, and Abakuá. There were three separate performance groups: one for Congo music and dance, one for Abakuá, and one for Yoruba, which I was part of. Later, the decision was made to unite these three groups into one, Conjunto Folklórico Nacional de Cuba, with dancers who were trained in the streets. For example, José Oriol Bustamante, from the Congo side, was a recognized palero (*tarero reconocido*). From the Abakuá side, there were serious practitioners – *negros sabios* (wise blacks) – who decided they were willing to contribute to the project. We were the Yoruba side: Jesús, Armandito, Estasio, Alfonsito, me, Trinidad.

Once the revolution was underway and the Conjunto Folklórico was founded in 1962, a lot of people wanted to be in the group. The competition was terrible; you had to really play to get in (*era terrible, había que machucar de verdad*). It wasn't a question of names: "I'm Carlos Aldama." No, no, no. You had to play. Only the best players were in the group. Jesús Pérez, Mario Aspirina, Julito. All the best. They invited about four hundred people to audition, and kept eighty-something. From there they selected the best and ended up with twenty or thirty group members. I actually began with the Conjunto as a dancer. But I quickly switched over to percussion, because much better dancers joined the troupe. But a good percussionist must know at least some dance and song. In that group there were folks who sang, danced, and played like hell (*con cojones*)!

Most all of the types that founded and directed the Conjunto had studied with Argelier León or with Fernando Ortiz. Ortiz was a *cabrón!* He was hip and quite a character. He would greet you like any Cuban, "¡Qué bolá! ¡Qué hay!" and so on. He would invite a lot of folks to his house to drink and eat, because he was rich. He lived right in front of the University of Havana. After everyone was a little drunk and had eaten well, he would say, "You know what so-and-so said? That you don't know anything about this or that ritual or legend . . ." And people would get indignant and begin to talk about what they knew of the African traditions. This is how he got a lot of his information. He was slick! He died soon after the revolution and they took over his materials. Through Trinidad Torregosa and Jesús Pérez, I got to be one of the drummers that illustrated the lecture-demonstrations these guys would put on with music and dance. We worked first with Ortiz, and later with León. Argelier León was one of Ortiz's main students, along with Alberto Pedro, who studied Abakuá, Rogelio Martínez Furé, who was into dance and theater and co-founded the Conjunto Folklórico Nacional de Cuba, and Miguel Barnet, who did the book *Biography of a Runaway Slave,* and who was initiated to Yemayá in Matanzas. He has had ocha for many years!

The Conjunto made its first tour of Europe in 1964. We left in April to play at the Bernal Theater in Paris, and we traveled on to Belgium and Spain before returning to Cuba. When we got back there were some problems and the directorship of the group shifted. One director, Marta Blanco, was dismissed and María Teresa Linares stepped in to replace her. María Teresa was Argelier León's wife and a scholar in her own right. This was 1965. Rogelio Martínez Furé was the ethnologist and consultant, Rodolfo Reyes Cortés (a Mexican) was the choreographer, and María Teresa Linares was the new general director. At the same time, new dancers were brought in. They came from other troupes and through auditions held in Centro Habana. This was the new generation of dancers for the Conjunto. Emilio O'Farrill, Julio Moba, José Oriol Bustamante, and other original members retired. Jesús Pérez left the group to play with Danza Moderna, leaving me in charge as the musical director of Conjunto Folklórico. When María Teresa came, she started to create distinctions of quality and rank between the dancers. All of us who had founded the group were from the streets – *santeros, paleros,* dock workers, humble people. None of us were trained dancers from the university. The original dancers were being ranked as "gray" dancers, which meant they were inferior to the new dancers in the group. Rodolfo Reyes

Cortés (the choreographer) said it himself: "The old ones were paid with that first tour in 1964." Now they were about to be out. That's where the problems started.

To me these new rules were racist. One of the musicians actually shot María Teresa behind this. The guy was Abakuá and a drummer, my friend's husband. He also had Ogun made. María Teresa classified him as a *gray dancer*, not a very good ranking at all. And the Conjunto was preparing for a national tour in 1966. He would be saying, "Check out how these folks are calling us 'gray' so that we can't go on the tour . . . I'm not gray, I'm black! I'll show them . . ." He got a hold of a gun and *ya tú sabes*.

One day she gave him three pieces of advice: 1) *No dejes camino por vereda* (Stick to what you know, don't lose your day job), 2) *No te metas en lo que no te importa* (Mind your own business), and 3) *No partas por la primera* (Look before you leap). When he heard this, he said, "Is that so?" pulled out his gun, cocked it, and shot her three times in the knee! Rodolfo came in the room and Miguelito shot him too! He got hit in the back and played dead. Another dancer's throat got messed up because of shrapnel or a stray bullet. Miguelito got twenty-four years in prison for all that. We appealed a few times and his sentence got reduced. But after this, people would joke and say that if you were part of Conjunto Folklórico it meant you were crazy.[19]

When we traveled we were paid something like twenty dollars a day. Close to nothing. We would work for the Conjunto until three in the afternoon, then do private classes, and even play at a cabaret by night in order to make a little extra money. There were some problems on that first tour in 1964. Some guys got drunk and stole and even hunted some ducks at the hotel. Rogelio Paris started saying that the problems happened because the group members were black. He was an asshole from a rich family and a racist. Blacks don't know how to act, *los negros* this, *los negros* that.

María Teresa Linares came in soon after. The last time I saw her was when she was directing the Museo de la Música, which was next door to the Bodeguita del Medio. The journal *Gaceta de Cuba* had just started to be published and she invited me, "Come see what I have," and it was a set of batá drums. I said, "Congratulations," and kept stepping! She was

A still image from the film *Historia de un ballet* by director José Massip, 1961. Carlos Aldama is drumming in the center of the frame and Lázaro Ros sings in the top right corner. *Courtesy of Carlos Aldama.*

asking for my help to identify drums. I told her to remember her three pieces of advice. She was a racist.[20] Later she became director of the Institute of Music and a recognized musicologist.

ORICHA MUSIC ONSTAGE AND IN REAL LIFE

I was part of a documentary film called *Historia de un ballet* by José Massip, which shows the process of making choreographer Ramiro Guerra's piece *Changó and Ogun,* based on Yoruba folklore. It shows the research process that he went through, beginning in the Afro-Cuban *toques* (religious celebrations with music) and ending up on the concert stage. Near the start of the film, Jesús Pérez, Andrés Isaaqui, and others play batá in the town of Regla. Then it shows a *güiro* party in Havana where I'm playing conga drums along with Trinidad Torregosa, Lázaro Ros, and

Carlos Aldama (left) with Lázaro Ros, 1990. *Photo by Calvin Holmes.*

others. This was done in 1961 before the Conjunto was even founded yet. The documentary shows the roots and then the final product, the stage production.

There is a danger in performing the oricha tradition on stage; you have to be careful not to lose touch with the roots. In what sense? Simply this. We rehearsed with a lot of people . . . like Lázaro Ros.[21] He became a great *cantador de santo* (oricha singer). He was a great *diloggun* reader also, an *obá*. He was damn good (*empingao*)! Ocha Güeye taught him how to do it. But Lázaro became an *artista*. He recorded an album on a radio station in Paris. That was his first recording. But there's one reality;

what is it? Either you are or you aren't, *olvídate*. The more you give and work within the religion, the more you will accomplish.

Some people forgot about the religion and embraced the stage.[22] They lost touch with the source. I've never done that. I have never brought the religion to the stage. What I have done is to take *elements from the religion* for use in the theater. The difference is in my behavior, my state of mind, my intention. Some people would give me a hard time, saying I was selling out the religion by doing stage performances. One guy who used to mess with me that way, I got him good. He had become military brass, which meant he could not be Abakuá, but he was. One day I ran into him at a lodge meeting. He told me not to say anything, and I reminded him of his comments, and we laughed! Your culture is with you all the time. We all create it together. You, me, and the other guy. I worked from 1959 to 2000 with the Ministry of Culture. I ended up being the musical director of the Conjunto. But I played actual toques every day. I was initiated to Changó on March 13, 1971, even though the government officials had confiscated my animals. During my forty-one years working with the Ministry of Culture I never stopped participating in actual ceremonies. With Jesús's drum we would play six or seven times each week. When my hands would hurt I used to pee on them. But it wasn't so bad. Only the first stroke at the start of the toque was painful; after that I wouldn't feel anything else.

For example, I always played in the Yemayá processions in Regla. There were two houses and each had its own procession. The one I participated in belonged to Susana Cantero. The other belonged to Pepa Herrera (Echu Bi), whose father was a babalawo from Africa. He was so important that other slaves purchased his freedom. At Susana's house on the hill in Regla is where we used to play. Her saints were stored right there in her house. The procession itself started at the church of Regla. Each of the two houses marched with its own statue of the Virgin of Regla. The reason for the procession was to salute the homes of the various santeros, and the route would change from year to year. We would meet at the old cemetery. Pepa's procession would take off in one direction and Susana's would take off in another. We had different routes, but it was on the same day, September eighth. We would meet back at the new cemetery in Regla. And from there again everyone went their own way. [Laughter as the next story comes to him.] Susana had a huge virgin, Pepa had small statues of the virgins and they walked slowly. Susana's big virgin was carried by a few guys and moved faster.

Trinidad Torregosa was the lead drummer of Pepa's procession. First Pablo had been the boss (*el jefe de todo el mundo*). But at this point, when I started to go, Pablo would be around somewhere having a good time (*jodiendo*). Jesús was the lead drummer for Susana Cantero. We used to play the Ibaloke rhythm during the walk in between houses where we saluted the santeros. And by the time we would cross Perdomo Street, everybody would take off with us and only the drummers and the saints themselves would be left with Pepa's procession! We would be singing *Donache* [vocal drum sounds] while Pepa was singing *Ibarago mojubara*, old stuff (*cosas antiguas*). People would hear us and say, ¡*Adiós, Pepa!*

[LISTEN TO TRACK 10]

From Perdomo we would take off up the hill (*subiendo la loma*); by six in the afternoon we were back at Susana's house and Pepa's procession had returned to hers. We started at seven in the morning. It was all day. The santeros we saluted would come and *dar coco* at the front door of their homes. [He invites me into the shrine room to show me a picture.] Let me show you a photograph of Susana's cabildo. There's my brother Alfonsito, this is me [back turned away from camera], El Ñato who had Ogun made, this is Andrés Isaaqui, who was an old drummer from Pablo's day. Way in the corner you have the famous ocha singer Eugenio de la Rosa (Odu Fora). This here is Susana Cantero's daughter, Almeyra. When I started going to the processions, Susana had already been dead for about five years. Her daughter, whom they also called La Mora, was in charge then. What they're doing is feeding the Bay of Havana (*se le está dando de comer*). That was the first thing we did before leaving the church. We gave coconuts and candles. But before that, earlier in the morning, they made sacrifice out in the middle of the Bay beyond the Morro of Havana.

We would go to the santeros' doors playing and singing. For example, a santera like La Negra would *dar coco* and pay a small *derecho* of

Yemayá Procession in Regla with batá drumming, circa 1957.
Prepared by Barbara Beckmeyer and Jeff McCall, 2010. Courtesy of Carlos Aldama.

maybe five cents. (Later she became a communist, left the religion, and then went crazy.) But this was an all day thing, a big party. And it would coincide with parties all over the town of Regla. So after the cabildo, it was still party time. For example, if you met a girl that day you would go off with her to have fun. Hundreds or thousands of people would participate in the procession. There were no toques anywhere that day. Drummers came all the way from Matanzas to be there. And there were so many women! Couples would split up before the procession and then get back together after it was done. You would have some beers, party at this Mexican-style club called Mar y Tierra, then go to the *posada* and make love. Since I had my wife, Santa, this would cause problems sometimes. She would show up looking for me, and *ya tú sabes!*

They stopped doing the procession a long time ago now. People stopped wanting to do it. After the revolution, Susana Cantero's daughter became brainwashed, put up the statues, and that was it for the procession. Later the government tried to bring it back with the Conjunto, but it didn't work. They tried to make it a folkloric thing, rather than the true religious event it had been. It didn't fly. Little by little, over time people lose their idiosyncrasies like that old ceremony. The oldest santeros stayed at home, they didn't come out anymore. So the ceremony was lost. The photograph that I showed you is from 1957 or 1958, before the triumph of the revolution. People still celebrate from September eighth into the ninth because that's the feast day for La Virgen de Regla.

In Regla there wouldn't be much trouble at the oricha parties or the Abakuá functions. The whites who lived there were Abakuá, santeros, and everything else, just like the blacks. They would kick your ass and you'd have to run to the dock and swim all the way back to Havana. That's right, after the beating you had to swim!

∗ ∗ ∗

You can bring the spirit with the drums alone. Or with just song. Jesús really had this one guy's number. As soon as he came around we would play *Taniboya* for Yemayá, nice and slow. He would start to dance, and before you knew it he would be spinning and our work was done, ocha was in the house. There was a priest of Changó that would get possessed whenever a lightning bolt struck. Boom! And Changó would come.

In the past, when there was a problem, you didn't have to call the oricha, because oricha would come on its own. Without singing, without drums, without anything. One time a man got mounted with Changó in Santiago de Cuba and came by bus – possessed! – all the way to La Habana to resolve a health problem. I swear to God. Take this herb, do this, do that, and then that was it, he went back to Oriente. But this was in the old days. No more. I think things like this change because of the young generation, lack of faith (*incredulidad*), vanity, and competition.

It's normal if you have a toque and no oricha came down. It wasn't common to pay people to come to dance ocha ceremonies. You would simply invite the santeros to come, they would ask permission of their oricha and come on. When I hear people say, "My Ochun will be dancing on Saturday," I can't help but think that it's bull. Back in the day when the oricha needed to come, it came on its own. No need for drums or songs or anything.

* * *

Jesús's drum was called Wa Lade (*Que venga la corona,* Bring the crown). Trinidad's drum was called Ako Bi Añá. A famous drum maker from Matanzas named Adofó made them.[23] He was very *receloso,* which means you had to convince him to tell you anything. I never met Adofó because he was even older than Pablo Roche. Before belonging to Trinidad, the drums had belonged to his brother Tareko, who was an *osainista,* a master of herbal medicine. For this reason he lived alone, as all osainistas do, because their shrine is so strong and intense.

The first time I heard the *Kan Kan* rhythm for the dead played was at Pablo Roche's burial, before the triumph of the revolution. There were several versions of this toque. After Pablo died, his drums got to be in really poor condition. There were a lot of problems. So what did Jesús do? He said, "Let's fix the drums." He took them back to his house, got them ready, and put on a toque for Pablo. Nasakó, Águedo Morales, and Jesús Pérez all played. Pedro Pablo "Aspirina" Valdez played too, and this was just before he passed on. Aspirina got the name because he would always be begging for an aspirin pill for a toothache or something. We would tease him, "Take the damn aspirin, man, but go see a doctor!" And the nickname *aspirina* stuck.

Remember Nasakó had been Pablo's favorite student. Nasakó didn't play with anyone else but Pablo. And when Pablo died he stopped playing. The last time Nasakó touched a drum was when Jesús put on that tambor for Pablo in Guanabacoa. That's when the guard began to change, just around the time of the revolution. There enters Papo Angarica, who had learned some from Nasakó, who did not teach many people. Papo and I started together. Papo with his father, and me with Jesús, you know?

I started to play *iyá* at about twenty years old. It was so hard to get Jesús to teach me, that when I finally started to learn I really took off. One time I was playing *itótele* for Jesús, and I was right with him, playing all the conversations he called for. After a while he told me to get up, but I didn't, I kept playing. He was pushing and pushing and I kept up with him. That's when he finally accepted me. He got up and sat me down on iyá. After that it was always iyá, for example in Conjunto Folklórico Nacional de Cuba. I taught a few other people in order to not have to play all the time myself. We rehearsed from 1 to 7 PM every day. First there was dance class, for technique, etcetera, and we would play conga or batá. First modern dance, then folklore. Then we would go over the choreographies.

As part of my work with Conjunto Folklórico I taught a lot of the drummers in Oriente. This was around 1965. They sent me there to learn *Tumba Francesa, Gagá, Vodú,* and other rhythms from eastern Cuba, and to teach the *santiagueros* batá. I taught Milián Galí in Santiago de Cuba. Later on Chachá from Matanzas made a set of fundamento for him. Galí liked to drink and was always full of laughter. He was a very accomplished musician. He led *La Conga de los Hoyos,* he sang, he was very good.

RECORDING ORICHA MUSIC

Jesús played with Merceditas Valdés, and so did I.[24] On that old recording of hers with *Mariwo Ye Ye Ye* it was Jesús, Armando Sotolongo, and me. I played okónkolo. We also played on the radio. I met her through Jesús. Trinidad taught her how to sing, but she didn't do bembés. Her thing was singing on shows like Radio Suaritos every Sunday. On these kinds of programs she would sing *cosas de santo* with drums, and so on.

Merceditas was so pretty when she was younger! Everybody was after her. She eventually got together with Guillermo Barreto, who was a great drummer and musician, the type of guy we used to call "*Americano*" because he was hip, wore American clothes, and the whole nine yards. He was with Orquesta de Música Moderna, which later became Irakere.[25] His brother had died because he was supposed to have Changó made, but his madrina, who could not make Changó, made him for Oyá instead. After that, Guillermo hated everything to do with *la religión*. He even stopped Merceditas from singing oricha music. Merceditas's mother had Changó and her father had Obatalá. Mercedes herself was a daughter of Ochun and she needed to make ocha. So once when Guillermo was away on tour in Czechoslovakia, she did it. When he came back and saw her he asked, "What have you done?" She said she had made santo.

* * *

I played batá with Sergio Vitier.[26] I was a founding member of his Grupo Oru. It was created in Sala Cadena. Sergio was a great guitarist. His brother, José María, was a great pianist. His father, Cintio Vitier, had been a great musician before him. Sergio played so beautifully. Often as we sat and talked I would ask him to play something from the Concierto de Aranjuez.[27] Or I would even pay to go see him at concerts.

Sergio had certain yearnings to experiment with different kinds of music. He had been a founding member of cutting-edge ensembles like Grupo de Experimentación Sonora,[28] Orquesta de Música Moderna, etcetera, but what he really wanted was to try out the music he had in his head. His music was never really accepted, though. People didn't like it that much. Not that it was bad; it was just too far out for most folks. It wasn't danceable for one thing. It was for listening. We would play at the National Theater, at Hotel Nacional, and similar places, while people were having dinner. He played his own compositions and meanwhile folks would eat. But sometimes he would play a *son* and people would get up and dance.

So he created Grupo Oru to play his music mixed with Yoruba things, collaborating with Rogelio Martínez Furé. For example, we would do a rhythm for Ochun with batá, and Vitier playing guitar. We recorded a lot; usually not whole albums, but small bits for different uses, some soundtrack pieces for films, etcetera. We played for the famous Cuban painter Wilfredo Lam in Paris when he died. He was from Sagua la Grande in Cuba and belonged to a well-known cabildo there called Kunalumbu. He asked his wife to have a group of musicians play folkloric music as they spread his ashes. Sergio Vitier made arrangements for Jesús Pérez, Rogelio Martínez Furé, Alberto Villareal, and me to travel to France to play for Wilfredo. We played a little bit of everything, from batá to Cuban lullabies.

FAMILY

How many times have I been married? Only once. But I have had three important women in my life. Are you doing some kind of interview? Do you intend to do some kind of biography of my life?! No. No. The day I decide to do that I'll do it myself, for me. *Mira,* there are moments in life, situations . . . The women I've had; I lived many years with all of them, many years together (*juntos*). I've done wrong like any man (*como qualquier cabrón*). But going from here to there like a butterfly, no. I was never the type to have a whole bunch of women. My main woman and a girlfriend, that's it (*mi esposa y una novia, ya*). I met my first woman, Santa, a long time ago (*hace una pila de años*), around 1953, before I became a drummer. She was with me all along and is the mother of my three daughters. My last child, my son Michel, was by my second partner Librada, who was a dancer and had Ochun made. I was with Librada for twenty-eight years, until she died four days before making a visit to the U.S. with the Conjunto in 1994. *Ya tú sabes* . . . these are parts of one's life (*parte de la vida de uno*). I have four children in all: Michel and Maida, who both live in New Jersey now, Dalia and Iliana, who still live in Havana. All have *santo hecho*. Michel has Obatalá, Maida has Ogun,

Dalia Eleguá, and Iliana has Changó. Plus I have five grandchildren! I met Yvette, my current partner and the only official wife I've had, at La Peña Cultural Center when she was still an *iyawó* and I liked her. After that we've never left each other's side. A lot of people thought we wouldn't last, not even three months. Especially being two children of Changó. But, *mira*, here we are.

I first started working with Jesús in Cabaret Tropicana before the revolution. There we played conga for the stage shows. When the revolution came Jesús and I both went to work with the group Danza Moderna with the great choreographer Ramiro Guerra. During that time I had to go into the army and even fought in the Bay of Pigs. I was a long-distance trucker so I was responsible for transporting arms and food. On April 17, 1960, the invaders landed in Cuba and on the next day it was full war. Everybody in combat! When the invasion happened, I was commanded to transport supplies. I would drive to the Morro Cabaña in Old Havana to load up with food, water, bullets, and whatever was needed. We would then take these things to the Australia sugar refinery, which is on the southern coast of Matanzas Province near Playa Larga (Long Beach) where the Bay of Pigs invasion took place. I had weapons and everything but I did no shooting. Even though I was not in open combat, I felt fear. With bombs dropping all around the place, who wouldn't? My brother Antonio was in the 119th Battalion and my father was in the 139th, which were the ones that transported the captured invaders to Havana. I was in the 134th Battalion. After the Bay of Pigs I remained for a time as just a driver.

Danza Moderna went on tour to France and Russia in 1960/61. I couldn't go because I was in the army. Jesús was mad because he was looking for me to rehearse for the trip. Once, during the time I drove trucks for the military, I went to an Abakuá celebration on the sixth of January. I didn't know much about the tradition, just the name of the *potencia* I belonged to. I went into the lodge with my green uniform and beret, and everybody just looked at me. They thought I must be an infiltrator or crazy. It was Chachá, the drummer, who saved my skin when he spoke up for me. *¡Tremenda toalla me tiró!* He was present in La Habana when I was sworn in, so he knew for sure. If you go to an Añá toque and something like this happens, you mention the drum(s) you were sworn to. I was sworn to Wa Lade and Ako Bi Añá.

THE SUGAR HARVEST OF 1970

The sugar harvest of 1970 was called "la zafra de los diez millones" because it was supposed to be ten million tons of sugar. The workers from all the *ministerios* in Cuba (the Ministry of Culture where I worked and all the others) went to cut cane. There were "Million ton brigades" throughout the island to coordinate the work, because the harvest had to be ten million tons! Cuba never used to burn the cane as a way to shorten the cutting process. But this time, in order to meet such a big goal, we did. All of us musicians and dancers from Havana were sent to work beyond the city limits in the countryside near a sugar refinery called Habana Libre. Each group worked in its own camp; Conjunto Folklórico over here, Danza Moderna over there, Pello el Afrokan in another area. Even the ballerinas from the Ballet Company got out there. They would walk around a bit in the fields early in the morning before the sun got hot and before long they would be gone home. Violinists too, for example, didn't cut much cane because they had to take care of their delicate wrists and such. So . . . *ya tú sabes* . . . it was us, *los negros* from Conjunto Folklórico Nacional who cut cane like animals.

We were stationed out there for about three months, June, July, and August. Sometimes I would get away and come home at night even though I wasn't supposed to. But in the end Cuba never did produce the ten million tons of sugar. It was a big disappointment and even a fiasco. But at least one good thing came out of the huge build up. The government and all the people were repeating the phrase *¡Los Diez Millones Van Van!* (The ten million tons must be achieved!) in order to build morale. A young musician called Juan Formell took the last part of that phrase, Van Van, to name his new group. Thanks to the harvest of 1970, Cuba's most famous dance band got its name, Los Van Van!

FIDEL

Mira, chico, let me tell you something. If Fidel doesn't have *santo* made – which I don't think he does – he definitely has a lot of babalawos working for him. On the ranch where he grew up he was always hanging around Haitian peasant workers who planted the sugarcane and coffee there. Fidel's father Ramon never looked at these people as slaves, he gave them some respect. Fidel was always in the *baracones* (workers' quarters), carrying on with the black women and what not. Around the singing and all the things those folks did. Through all the attempts on his life some miraculous things have happened. Once they threw a grenade at him and he caught it. It even exploded, but he was totally unharmed. So in my opinion he's protected by quite a bit of magic (*bastante brujería*).

In 1964 Fidel showed up unannounced at Teatro Mella while Conjunto Folklórico was performing. He was attracted by the crowd outside. He decided on the spot that the Conjunto would go on a trip to play Paris. It was a big thing, because up until then only the ballet, the modern dance troupe, etcetera, were scheduled to go.

WAR IN ANGOLA

During the military participation in Angola, all races of Cubans went. White, black, and *mulato.* If you didn't go, government officials would mark your *carnet* (ID card) with a red slash. You could lose your job and all kinds of opportunities would be closed to you. You had the right to refuse to go, but if you said no you were sure (*seguro, seguro*) to get that red slash, which meant "This guy's no good!" [laughter] *Ay muchacho,* all kinds of tragedies took place in Cuba over that kind of thing. Some people did in fact refuse to go. They would defend *Cuba,* but felt like Angola was not their fight. Folks would say, "Those people over there have done nothing to me." (*Si esta gente no se metieron conmigo.*) And they lost their jobs. So at the meetings the officials would ask, "Who is going to volunteer?" And even if they didn't really want to go, people's hands would go up.

Some came back with strange illnesses. One friend had to be quarantined and you could only talk to him through glass. I went to Angola in 1984 as a musician and to do whatever was needed (*como músico y en función de todo*). I never went deep into the forest in Angola (*la selva*) because I didn't stay long. After only fifteen or twenty days I got sick with a bad case of malaria. I started to throw up, my legs got weak, and I started to sweat. When I went to the military doctor I discovered that it was a guy I knew from Havana who always used to ask me to teach him to play drums. The prescription he gave me was two bottles of pure alcohol each day along with some horrible tasting pills. I mean these pills were terrible. But, imagine that for medicine, two bottles of alcohol. The guys wanted me to give them malaria so they could have the same treatment! After a short time they sent me back to Cuba. They told me to keep my mouth shut, and put me on a first-class flight alongside government officials returning to Havana.

THE SPECIAL PERIOD AND THE DRUM

After Jesús died in 1985, I withdrew (*me quité*), because there were problems. Most people loved money, but I loved Jesús. *El amor y el interés fueron al campo un día, y más pudo el interés que el amor que le tenía.* I wanted to kill his son. But I knew Jesús wouldn't have liked that, and I didn't want to upset his spirit. I couldn't stand his daughter either. She was bad too. Like a lot of others she became a communist and renounced her oricha. A lot of the people who fought over controlling the drums (Wa Lade) ended up dying from it, because they don't know how to manage such strong spirits like Añá and Osain (*no saben andar con eso*).

The procession for Jesús's funeral went down Zanja Street to the police headquarters, a few blocks away. *¿Qué pasó?* When Jesús died everybody wanted what should have been mine. This was traditionally decided by descent: when Trinidad died the drums went to Jesús, when he passed they should have come to me. But certain people fought for the drums because they wanted to make money. They loved money more than they loved Jesús. Regino was the one who ended up with Wa Lade. Papaíto wanted to be the chief. But he didn't have the right character for it. Armandito wanted to as well but he couldn't do it either. So it was Regino. Folks were into boasting that they were the owner of Jesús's drums. They started making a lot of drums for foreigners. Regino said to

Carlos Aldama drumming at Jesús Pérez's funeral, 1985. *Left to right,* Bárbaro Valdés, Ricardo Aldama (Carlos's cousin), Armando Pedroso (holding container), Gregorio "El Goyo" Hernández, Carlos Aldama, and Pancho Quinto. *Courtesy of Carlos Aldama.*

me about Jesús's drums: "This isn't mine, it's yours. These folks robbed you." If they had been given to me I would have cared for them and maintained the tradition. Where are the drums now? I don't even want to know. One day someone told me that if I saw Jesús's drums I'd be surprised and upset (*te caes pa' trás*). I went to Jesús's grave and assured him I had nothing to do with it. Like I said, *el interés y el amor fueron al campo un día.* But at least I'm still here! I have peace and I'm still playing.

After the first music and dance courses came out in Cuba, all kinds of different groups started offering classes, etcetera. It became big business. A lot of drummers from all over the world came to study in the courses put on by the Conjunto Folklórico.[29] First it was in the Escuela Nacional

Jesús Pérez as an old man, circa 1978. *Courtesy of Carlos Aldama.*

Carlos Aldama with drummers in Cuba, 1990. *Left to right,* Julio "Botella," unknown drummer with head down, Miguel López, Ángel Bolaños, Yagbe Gerrard, Regino Jiménez, and Carlos Aldama. *Photo by Calvin Holmes.*

de Arte and many of the students were from California. A lot of North Americans were bringing student groups to Cuba. They came to party and have sex. But they did business and studied music and dance too. Baba Duru's wife, Carolina, the one with Ochun made, she brought students as well during this time. Later the course moved over to Conjunto Folklórico. Lastly the courses began at Danza Moderna. I met Yagbe because he went to Conjunto classes. Baba Duru as well. Yagbe is the one who has studied with me the most.

For a long time I did not feel much desire to teach. Everybody was at each other's throats to get and keep students. It was a drag! So I didn't get into it. This was the early nineties. Since I was independent and could go abroad from time to time, or play at Cabaret Tropicana, I didn't get too mixed up in it. Someone would come to study with me for a certain price, then some other drummer would steal them by charging less money. It's forty dollars an hour if you want to study with me. If that works for you, fine. If not, it's fine too. To give you an idea of what it was like, one time I was walking down Belascoaín Street in Centro Habana and a guy came up to me and yelled, "Carlos, you're alive!" and I said, "Hell yeah, I'm alive." "But they told me you were dead." People were that cold! A student would show up and ask for you and they'd say, "He's dead, study with me."

That's how they would take away your students. But I didn't care. During this time people came to study with me from Holland, Italy, and other countries. After the Conjunto classes is when I would give private lessons. In the schools I also did special workshops and individual lessons. I also traveled. I went to Holland to teach. There are probably people there still playing what they learned. I went to Switzerland, France, and Italy too. In 1997, Michael Kramer brought me to teach in the U.S., at the New College on Valencia Street.

It's like what happened with one of my students who came to Cuba. When he made his second trip to Cuba and came looking for me, they told him I was out of the country. Get this! They initiated him into *ocha, Ifá,* and made him a set of sacred batá drums (*le hicieron santo, Ifá, y tambores de fundamento*). All the while he's asking where I am . . . Then one day I'm relaxing on the Malecón near Hotel Riviera, having a drink, and a guy comes up and asks me, "Hey, when did you get back?" I said,

"From where? I've been sitting right here!" José had left that same day, still looking for me.

AÑÁ AND VIOLENCE

In Santería people don't look at your sexual preference. In Abakuá they do. In Santería they did not look into your personal life that way. In Abakuá you've got to be a man, drummers/omo Añá must be men; a palero must be a man, in any sacred musical instrument, from batá drums to Iyesá drums, you've got to be a man to play. By this I mean heterosexual. But in Santería no one asks if you are a man or not. All are welcome. In Añá, the question of what manhood meant became a problem. This was one of the reasons why I started fading off the scene. Why? Because if you're not a tough guy or don't like to fight, somebody might call you a punk and say you can't be sworn to the drum to play Añá.

One time I got beat up by a guy, one of my brother's friends. I was all dressed up and clean one afternoon on the Malecón and I asked the guy to let me pass as he washed his car. When I walked by he wet me and I challenged him to a fight. He studied boxing and karate and judo and everything else. He body slammed me and hurt my whole side. (*Me metió un estrallón de pinga.*) I swore I would kill him. But when I saw him again one day in San Leopoldo with members of comparsa La Borrachita I decided it was better to let it go and not fight, because I didn't want any part of him! And for this situation, my not wanting to fight, you think they could say I was gay and shouldn't be allowed to play the drum? This all started happening in the 1980s and 1990s. Añá became more gangsterish than Abakuá. I was never into this. I was but I wasn't. I began to fade out. Jesús had always said, "No gangsters here . . . guapería only with the drum. Wear a little gold, a PR shirt, a nice pair of shoes, be able to buy a round of beers for your friends." This was positive *guapería*. So I stopped going to *juramentos* (initiations) because they came to be dangerous, like any popular dance at La Tropical or La Polar.

In Cuba the *categoría* of tambolero (the respect due to drummers) has been lost. They used to make arrangements for you to play on a certain day, they would ask you what you wanted to eat. It was elegant treatment. But at a certain point it changed. Even a person with means might serve the drummers *picadillo de soya*. My son, who's crazy, would say, "Eggun!" signaling that the ritual meal was done, meaning that he refused to eat such poor food. You would have to give two coconuts, two candles, a bottle of rum, and a *derecho* (money offering) in payment days or weeks *before* the toque if you wanted Añá to play.

Jesús's son Kimani even wanted to learn from me but I told him no. "My father taught you," he said, "so I'd like for you to teach me." At first I said okay. I even gave him an *okónkolo* to practice at home. Later on he explained that he was a medical student preparing to be a surgeon. When I found this out I went and took the drum back. I explained to him that he couldn't be a surgeon and play batá; his hands couldn't be swollen and shaking when it was time to operate on someone. Besides, it was better for him to be Doctor Kimani Pérez, omo Ochun, than to be the drummer Kimani Pérez, who'd like to be a surgeon but can't, because his hands are too swollen! [laughter] He got upset at first, but he had to accept it.

LEAVING CONJUNTO FOLKLÓRICO AND IMMIGRATING TO THE UNITED STATES

On my recent visit to Cuba I did not go and visit anyone from Conjunto Folklórico Nacional. Either they love you or they don't. They retired me at a time when I felt I still had more to give. So after that I haven't been back. In 1990 they said, "Carlos you'll be more productive in the schools outside of Cuba working alone." They said it was necessary to make way for the youth (*abrir paso a la juventud*). This was Alberto Villareal speaking, who was the director of percussion, even though he couldn't really play. Imagine a drummer in the world of Cuban folklore who can't even play *quinto*. They used to call him ol' heavy hands (*mano torpe*) because he was so slow. So, anyway, I said okay. I left and went about teaching private lessons and teaching abroad. That eventually led to my coming to the States. (Later, my son Michel worked with Conjunto Folklórico too.)

I first visited the U.S. in 1980. Conjunto Folklórico did a tour of the East Coast – New York, Washington, D.C. In the early 1990s I went to Italy, Mexico, Switzerland, Holland, and France (Paris) by myself to teach at universities and all different kinds of schools. I worked at the University of Mexico. I worked in the Philharmonic and also in the Zona

Rosada district in Mexico City. In Italy, in Rome, I worked at what they call the Timba School (*Escuela de Timba*). It was good for me.

I'm here in the U.S. right now thanks to Changó. The last time I played Jesús's drums in Havana, Changó came up to me and told me to sit down and play for him. At this point I hadn't played Jesús's drums for a while and I wasn't on good terms with the other drummers, so I hesitated. But Changó was stern, "As your father I command you to play for me now!" So I played Bajuba and Meta. After he had danced a long time, he stopped and said, "Now you are going to go and play 'on the other side'" (*del otro lado*). Shortly after that I found myself in San Francisco!

In 1997, I came to California, invited by Michael Kramer to teach at the New College in San Francisco. The Institute of Music in Cuba sent me. I stayed about three years on this first long visit. When I got back to Cuba in 2000 they said they had been waiting for me. "*¡Véte pa' la pinga!*" they said . . . I was out. I didn't know why, and it hurt. They had known where I was and everything had been above board, arranged by the well-known lawyer Bill Martínez. When I arrived in Cuba I had a return visa to go back to the U.S. I explained that I had students waiting to study with me in California. I even had a transition visa to go through Mexico.

The Cuban officials said, "Okay, but you need a certified letter from the foreign airline verifying your travel plans." What?! No one has ever heard of this requirement, this letter! I said okay. I was already disconnected from the Ministry of Culture, so I didn't need any approval from them. I was standing right in front of the offices of Mexicana Airlines. I asked if they had a ticket to Mexico. It was six o'clock in the afternoon and the flight was leaving at three in the morning. I had my visa to get through Cancun. So I grabbed a bag and took off! I was already out of the Conjunto and out of the Ministry of Culture. If I stayed I would never have been able to leave Cuba. That was in 2000 and I've been here in California ever since. How could they require a certified letter for me to travel!? *Yo soy perro viejo, muchacho.* I'm an old dog, man, and I had to show them that.

4

Diaspora

Diaspora entails continuity and change, harmony and dissonance, familiarity and foreignness. When I think of my study with Carlos I am inspired by the possibility of reaching back into my own ancestral past through the drum – its transcendental musical beauty and its historical lineage. Our experiences together often evoke for me a deep feeling of unity within the African Diaspora. However, many of Carlos's experiences traveling the world reveal the limits of identification between diaspora groups and force us to acknowledge real conflicts. In this chapter Carlos tells of his adventures as a traveler and performer in Africa, Europe, Latin America, the Caribbean, and the United States. His most detailed stories are about his experiences as a batá drummer in the Bay Area of California.

Traveling in Africa, Carlos was fascinated that the Yoruba he learned in Cuba (the Yoruba brought by his ancestors a century earlier) was intelligible to contemporary Yoruba speakers in Africa. He greeted people, ordered food, and asked directions in Yoruba. He was surprised to learn that many Africans did not know about the trans-Atlantic slave trade that took millions of blacks to the Americas, to Cuba. In fact, they did not know where Cuba was. In other cases, the Africans knew about Cuba and identified the island with Fidel and revolution. Carlos delights in moments of recognition between Cubans and Africans, but these encounters do not translate into sustained, transformative cultural exchange for either group.

Carlos shows that Cubans often struggle to separate themselves from the politics and revolutionary identity of their nation. In Panama, when authorities mistreated group members because they disagreed with Fidel's policies, Carlos's identity as an oricha priest was a saving grace. Because he is a priest of Changó, he could avoid being totally and only identified with Fidel. His experiences moving throughout the African Diaspora also underscore the fact that it is mainly in the context of music and sports that black Cubans have the chance to travel the world.

* * *

Añá drumming batteries or ensembles are like professional guilds, where the actual drum tradition is passed from master teacher to apprentices. They offer rich opportunities to understand the evolution of the batá tradition, to comprehend the relationships between marginalized groups (like Latinos and African Americans in the United States), and to see how performance speaks volumes about history and culture in the context of the Black Atlantic. Carlos is engaged in what Mason calls "transcultural war," and knows it full well.[1] I am too, and perhaps so are all *bataleros*. The aim of the struggle, though, is not control for its own sake, but to ensure the continued life and health of the batá tradition. As dance anthropologist Yvonne Daniel writes, "Dance and music are central to a description of African American life; [they] interconnect and reference other dimensions beyond the social arena." She refers to political acts through performance that "vibrate with both spiritual and social ideals."[2] Batá drummers today, like Carlos Aldama, exhibit the ongoing and strong tensions that are characteristic within situations of continuity and change – in this case, among drummers and within the dominant, mainstream society that is at once racist and suspect of African religions.

On one hand, the descendants of enslaved Yoruba who play the batá in Cuba and other reaches of the diaspora continue to thwart the destructive intentions of their former masters. They see their main responsibility as providing their communities with traditional culture that will bolster worshipping practitioners and others in the onslaught of any future conquerors. They understand Añá and the batá as the representation of camaraderie and community. The drum is a metaphor for life. In Carlos's words, "It will be here tomorrow, we will die"; so today we should play with all our heart and teach. Maintenance of the batá tradition is a tremendous offensive counterattack in the transcultural war between "tradition" and "destruction."

On the other hand, there are tensions among Cuban batá drummers based on stylistic differences and perhaps a generation gap, and between Cuban and non-Cuban batá drummers (particularly African American) in the United States. These conflicts or clashes are based on even more complex issues. There are questions of authority and authenticity within transcultural wars, where two African-descended groups assert their statuses as heirs of those ancient Africans who came bearing the drum, and as viable leaders in the continued transculturation of the batá.

When Carlos makes the assertion that there are similarities and differences between him and me, between Cubans and African Americans, he hints at the definition of *diaspora* and speaks to one of the main themes of this book. He celebrates common roots at the same time as he acknowledges distinct, even conflicting, idiosyncrasies within each community. He is aware of tensions between various diaspora groups (for example, Cubans, African Americans, and Puerto Ricans), as the drum tradition is carried on and reshaped in the United States and elsewhere. A Nigerian is not a Cuban is not an African American is not a Puerto Rican. But all can be "Yoruba." They may not all "get along," but they are family.

Consider, for example, the differences between Carlos's and my relationship to the discourse of Yoruba unity, especially regarding the potential for tensions around questions of authenticity and authority between Cubans and African Americans (and white Americans). Carlos and other Cubans construct their relationship to Africa largely by narrating specific links, through sacred drums and their owners, to first-generation Africans in Cuba. He warns, "I carry what Cuba has given me." Like many African Americans, I forge my relationship to Africa partly through cultural reconstruction; in this case by recuperating, via Cuban expertise, drum practices and lineages that have been lost. Carlos even suggests that blackness is an advantage in the project of transmitting and preserving the batá tradition. But he balances that statement with the assertion that whites can be *santeros* (priests), consecrated drummers, and so on, just as well as blacks. Carlos's openness calls into question whether or not there is a special role for African Americans to play in carrying on the batá tradition in the United States. His views highlight the complex nature of transmitting cultural traditions, especially when refracted and reformed in diaspora.

The batá drum tradition arrived to the United States decades after the religion of Santería was already here. John Mason has written about the first batá ceremony in New York City in 1961, led by one of Carlos's contemporaries, Julito Collazo. In Carlos's view, the recent arrival of batá on these shores means that the tradition is much less developed and rich than in Cuba. For him there are too few toques to sustain the drum tradition – for aspiring drummers to learn, experienced players to practice and improve, and for masters to remember. Particularly in California, there are too many consecrated drums for such a relatively small community whose members throw so few toques. The result is that many *fundamento* drums sit mostly idle. Carlos's story shows that it is not easy to survive as a ritual drummer in the Bay Area, due to the very few toques that happen and the community's limited ability and willingness to recognize and support sublime eloquence over straight competence. Like *batalero* Felipe García Villamil in the book *Drumming for the Gods,* in order to make ends meet in the United States, Carlos is forced to hustle in other ways besides music.

Carlos laments the fact that the old way he was taught to play certain toques – like Kan Kan for the dead – is all but lost here. He also expresses concern about too much mixing of related, but distinct traditions, like Nigerian eggun masquerading and Cuban batá drumming. He suggests that if you don't know exactly what you are doing such blending can be useless or even dangerous. In addition, there is little attention to important protocol, like the ceremonial meal served to drummers before a ceremony. Instead of a feast served to them by a priestess of Ochun before playing, it's Kentucky Fried Chicken after the toque!

Carlos recognizes the complex issue of race in regard to the drum. He asserts that "it's not about race," that anyone can learn to play batá and play well. He also understands batá as an African tradition and believes that black people should be its primary caretakers. He makes the (for some) painful observation that many of the best batá drummers and ensembles that work the most in California are white and seem to even marginalize or exclude blacks. Carlos also notes that Cubans who came to the United States without knowing the drum usually do not learn. This may have a lot to do with the difficulty of making a living as a person of color and as an immigrant in this country. It is part of the same phenomenon that makes white folks more able than other groups to study consistently, travel to Cuba, and so on, in order to become versed in the drum liturgy, the religious tradition, and other practices.

The experiences of a particular drummer, Carlos Aldama, who has seen the shifts in the batá tradition both in Cuba and the United States, shed light on just what happens in particular spaces (between master and apprentice, within Añá battery ensembles, between the dancer and the drummer, as well as during ritual parties or *wemilere*) where the teaching and transformation of the batá drum liturgy happen. Many of the dynamics that are at play in this transculturation come from "outside the music," as community and individual experiences as people of color in Cuba and the United States bear upon the situations and relationships in question. *Who owns the tradition? Who knows more? What gives you the right? Who's baddd?!*

*   Carlos   *

You are African American. We are both from the same continent (America), and we both have ocha made. But you have your own culture because you were born here. Understand? We are in the same religion and we both play drums. But you carry inside of yourself what the U.S. experience has given you. I carry what the island of Cuba gave me.

AFRICA

I played music a few times in Angola and Ghana. But not with the Africans. I played a lot of rumba in the Cuban camp. We didn't play much with the Africans. The only thing we played in Africa with the Africans was *kimbisa,* which is a kind of Palo. A lot of great paleros like Emilio O'Farrill, José Oriol Bustamante, and Julito Moba were in the Conjunto.

They were famous paleros, recognized by everyone. There was one Cuban guy, Selvando Gutiérrez Cayo, my *compadre,* who had a *prenda de kimbisa.* When he would sing, the Ghanaians could understand. Once we were in a village of lion hunters in Ghana on the border with Nigeria doing our show. The people had rifles and some of them were painted up with stripes. When we were finished, the Africans started to play, and Selvando said, "Hey, that's kimbisa," and he started to sing with them. The Africans were totally surprised, and it became an exchange between the Cubans and the Africans. They even let him play their drums, which they usually did not do. They were crazy about us.

In this same town, I think it was called Benyatanga, I asked for food in Yoruba. Give me some *yucca,* give me this and that. They asked how I could speak and understand. I told them, I am a descendent of Africa. "Where are you from?" Cuba. "Where's Cuba?" Get out of town if you don't know! Cuba is one of the places where the most African slaves were taken.

We went around to different villages. Everywhere we went people would sacrifice a chicken at the door. If the chicken would fly a bit afterwards, then we could enter. If not, then we couldn't. We met lion hunters. We dined with the King of the Ashanti tribe. He was a young man, an official in the air force and president of the civil army. Part of our group traveled in his plane, a 757 jet. But some of us, including me, arranged to travel in a smaller plane, which took much longer. They arrived in one hour and we got there in six. We were in no hurry. We drank a lot of whiskey and played rumba all along the way. From there we went on to Mozambique and Zambia. Some folks would understand us perfectly; but others would not. In or around Nigeria the Africans could understand us because that's where a lot of Cuban culture comes from. But, of course, all Africans aren't Nigerian; so many could not understand our African talk from Cuba. Each town, each area has its own specific music and dance. But in a lot of villages they sang the kimbisa I mentioned earlier.

I never made it to Ile Ife in Nigeria. But Jesús did. He went with Danza Moderna to a festival in Lagos. He went to the Calabar and spoke Abakuá and folks would start to cry. Yes. Because Abakuá is from the

Calabar. For the most part it's been lost there, but it still exists in Cuba. Things kept on changing in Africa, but in Cuba things were maintained as they were. People would say, "Does this really still exist in Cuba? I want to go there!" Many of the gifts received by Cubans on these excursions to Africa became the main collection of the Casa de África museum in Havana.

LATIN AMERICA AND THE CARIBBEAN

It was in Jamaica that I first heard reggae. That's where I started to get into Bob Marley. I even began studying some electric bass to play that music. I went to Carnival on some English Caribbean island (I can't remember which) and I got lost following one of the floats that were playing reggae. I never saw any Santería or anything on the English Caribbean islands. I saw mostly Christianity and Rastafarianism. There are serious Rastas in these places. They drink rainwater and smoke plenty of marijuana. They're complete naturalists. In a lot of places people lived in houses on stilts. In the English Caribbean places like Belize and Guyana, they use steel drum bands. I love the steel bands too. Throughout my travels in Africa, Latin America, the Caribbean, and Europe I only played batá as an artist, never in ceremony. I never went to Haiti.

In Mexico and Venezuela there were many expatriate Cubans. There are many *santeros, babalawos,* and *tambores de fundamento* in Venezuela, for example. In Panama too. I was coming back to Cuba on a plane from somewhere in the Caribbean, and we had to stop in Panama because of a storm. When we got there, the Panamanians started to say stuff like, "You Cubans are sending your brothers to die in Angola!" and they refused to give us water or food. But I had on my *collares* (bead necklaces). And one of the Panamanian officials asked me if I was a santero. I said yes and explained that they were talking about political issues that had nothing to do with us, and that almost all of the other Cubans were santeros too. That at least got us some water.

I bought as many parrot feathers and thunder stones (*odun ará*) as I could get my hands on in Panama and the Dominican Republic. In Cuba these items are rare and valuable. People use the feathers to adorn new initiates, and the stones are for Changó. My wife made a lot of money selling those things when I got back to Havana. I never played music in cabarets in the Caribbean either. I would go out but just to have fun.

EUROPE

There were a lot of Africans in Europe! In Czechoslovakia, Hungary, etcetera, there were a lot of Africans. Like on the continent, they would often say, "We understand what you all are singing!" I only played cabaret gigs in Italy – Venice, Florence, Rome, Palermo, and other cities. I went to Italy once with the painter Manuel Mendive as well. They had burned a famous painting of his called El Cisne Blanco (The White Swan) in Miami. Since Mendive was associated with the highest echelon of the Cuban arts and letters scene, they suggested that he re-paint the piece while touring Europe on the way to the famous Biennale art show in Venice, Italy. We started off in London, then France, Hungary, Spain, and finally Italy. This was a six-month tour. We played the drums while Mendive would paint, in a kind of public performance. There were three female dancers. He would paint on their bodies and on canvas. We played Chachalokuafun or Ñongo on the batá so that the dancers would have something to move to. After the exhibit in Venice, I went home to Cuba because I missed my family.

　　I know Europe better than some millionaires. So I am very grateful to the Cuban Revolution. But it's fifty years now of eating with a ration book (*libreta*). And there's only about two channels on TV. Why can't Cuban youth live well like young people around the world?

THE UNITED STATES

I traveled to the U.S. for the first time in 1980 when I already had ocha made for nine years. I came to work with Conjunto Folklórico Nacional de Cuba on a tour to New York City (Brooklyn Center), Syracuse, Philadelphia, and Washington, D.C. We were in the U.S. until March 31. On April 4 the *marielitos* came. When I got back to Cuba everybody was telling me to leave, to go back to the U.S., people were screaming.

Before Mariel, it was the old santeros from Cuba – who had come in the 1950s and 1960s – who ran things in the U.S., not the *boricuas* (Puerto Ricans) like today. Everybody thought I would stay in the U.S. because before Mariel there were many santeros but no drummers, so there was a lot of work available. Puntilla, Coyude, and other drummers came with Mariel. In the U.S. they would tell me, "Don't leave, we have *babalawos* and everything, but we need drummers." Julito Collazo was the only one. He was a student of Jesús. He went to play with Jesús and was even able to play with Pablo Roche before he died. He started to learn with Jesús, and he was a cabrón. He was always putting people off the quinto in the comparsa saying they didn't know what they were doing. He couldn't say that to me, though, because I played quinto for Los Dandy de Belén. He came to the U.S. in the 1940s. I saw him in 1980. He had worked with Trinidad Torregosa and those guys, and I had seen him then. His last toque we played together in the Bronx in 1999. He died in 2004.

The *tambolero* who passed away most recently, in 2010, was Francisco Aguabella. I saw him only a few times in Cuba because he left the island when I was young and worked a lot in California. I saw him once when he visited Cuba and came to say hello to Trinidad Torregosa in Havana. I saw him in San Francisco in 1997 and he was asking me about the old tamboleros who had all died by that time. Francisco was more than ten years older than me. May the souls of all these drummers rest in peace. *Ibaé Tonú.*

* * *

Before, in Cuba, batá drummers were organized by groups (*por banda*). There was Jesús's battery, Fermin's battery, Nicolás's battery, and so on. Here in the U.S., in California, it's not that way. I tried to promote this kind of thing around here but it never caught on. The only battery I have played with consistently here in the U.S. belongs to Piri Ochun. In my life here he's been like another Jesús for me, because he brought back the old Carlos who was always around the drum. With everybody else I feel like I'm in the way. Everybody wants to be the boss so I stay away. No

Left to right, Carlos Aldama, Piri Ochun, and David Frazier, 2007.
Courtesy of Randy Rosso.

one can tell me much about Añá because I paid my dues in Cuba. *Cada gallo canta en su patio.* Every person runs things in their own home. But with Piri it's been like family.

I met Piri in 1997 about five days after I arrived in San Francisco. Between 1985 when Jesús died and 1997, I had been practically retired from playing batá. I only played from time to time with Pedrito Saavedra's drum. But generally, I wasn't interested. Regino Jiménez and others would say, "Come play with us, these drums are your drums." But I didn't want to. So it was through Piri in California that I got back into batá. At that time the only people with consecrated batá drums in the Bay Area were Piri, Michael Spiro, and Yagbe. Piri put me to work immediately. The first thing we did was an *ebbó* for an ocha ceremony. (I worked as an *obá* and led the proceedings.) Then it was off to Los Angeles, and on and on. I became the iyá player and leader of his drum battery, which included David Frazier, Bernard Wray, Piri's son Damian, Chris "Flaco"

Los Tambores Batá Oba Yororo Eleri Oba, 2001. *Standing left to right,* Bernard Wray, Piri Ochun, Chris "Flaco" Walker, and Sekou Gibson; *seated,* Damian de Jesús, Carlos Aldama, and David Frazier. *Courtesy of Carlos Aldama.*

Walker, and Sekou Gibson. My heritage as an old *tambolero* from Cuba helped establish Piri's *fundamento,* called Oba Yororo Eleri Oba.

There is an oricha community here in the Bay Area, but you can't really feel it. We need to come together more. The toque yesterday at Piri's house was great because people needed it. He is the one that plays the most out here, and this is the first toque he put on in a while. Here in the U.S. people have all kinds of different interests in the music. For some drumming is a hobby, some just like to play a little every now and again. Some won't come around unless you give them a special invitation. The whole thing is just different. You have to make a pact with yourself to play at a certain level at all times, even if you are playing with weaker drummers who may be learning from you. Know what the level is and go there. Each country has its own way. Here in the U.S. we don't play much batá. Here nobody provides *el almuerzo,* the ritual meal for drum-

Carlos and Yvette Aldama, 1999. *Courtesy of Chris Walker.*

mers. The distance (*la lejanía*) from Cuba is a serious thing. There are too many drums and everybody is confined to their own house or their small circle of associates. People don't see each other (*la gente no se ve*), and it's making the tradition disappear all by itself.

Because the community is so small, I don't play every day. I play when you come for lessons, or when there's some activity going on. For example, I play conga very rarely now. Maybe if I'm at Piri Ochun's house or in the rumba at La Peña and someone pushes a conga in my face. But otherwise I don't play. Why should I kill myself practicing all that if I have nowhere to use it?

* * *

Here in the San Francisco Bay Area, there is a lot of *desconocimiento*, lack of knowledge. This is true in New York and Los Angeles too, but especially here in the Bay Area. Not just regarding the drums, but the whole religious system of Santería. The community is smaller and there's less information. It's where the least number of toques and other kinds of ceremonies happen. In L.A. and New York there are more opportunities to learn and develop as individuals and as a community. For example, there are very few eggun toques here in California. Just the other day I went to what might have been my first ever in this area. Some people do ceremonies that come close, but they are so different from what I learned in Cuba that they don't count. But, when in Rome . . . (*Pero al pueblo que llegues, lo que vieres.*) It's not that I know much more than anyone else, but at least I was taught.

The Kan Kan for the dead is played only for Las Honras (La Zonra), only then. It's played where you do La Saraza for eggun. You have to play this for accomplished santeros that have four or more godchildren. You have to have a ceremonial meal where you do a ceremony called Levantar el Mantel (clearing the table cloth). Sometimes people will play and sing for eggun to honor a special person. But unless they have enough godchildren, you don't do the Mantel, you don't play the whole set of eggun rhythms.

One time Papo Angarica, Nasakó, Luis Santa María . . . a group of guys went to a Youth Festival in Algeria I think it was. They went on a boat in 1965 or 1966, and on the way Nasakó started rehearsing with Papo. By the time they came back, they had come up with a bunch of *inventos* within Kan Kan. Some of them started saying to those of us who still played the old way that, "This *tambor* doesn't go that way." Jesús would look at me and say, "Hogwash, that's not what Pablo Roche taught us. Don't change!" I don't waste my time anymore trying to explain things to people. People do what they like and I keep my mouth shut. Not many people around here play this toque. Many of those who do, play it differently from the way I was taught.

One time here in California they were going to do a toque for eggun and they wanted to use masked dancers like in Africa. I threatened to leave, because that's not what we do in Cuba. You can't ask me to come and sing as they do in Cuba, then come out with elements from another system. [laughing] Do that by yourself. Don't call me!

WHITE FOLKS

Everybody has their own *política,* their way of doing things. Jesús had his own. Nicolás Angarica, and so on. I don't really know Spiro's *política,* but he is the one who plays the most out here. Like Puntilla. May he rest in peace, that's who played the most in New York. For every five times Coyude's drum plays, Puntilla's plays thirty times! Spiro's battery is arguably the best in California, because the drummers are consistent. The other groups are looser, less polished. Back in the day in Cuba, almost no whites played batá. They started to play through Jesús.[3] With the development of the revolution and the Conjunto Folklórico Nacional more whites began to learn batá. And they played well. Why not? Look at Flaco (a white American) who studied with many different teachers and plays well. There are millions of blacks in Cuba who can't even play clave! So go figure; it's not about race (*no mires el color*).

MONEY

I haven't had much luck earning money here. I have been misunderstood. I never came here thinking about pushing other drummers out to take their place (*quítate tú pa' ponerme yo*). People would say that in order to earn money I would have to leave the Bay Area. But it was Piri who opened the way for me. Economically, I was never very demanding of him (*nunca fui mentalista con él*). But he was always generous with me. We had the most work in the late 1990s and early 2000s. But after that, there have been fewer and fewer toques for us to play.

Carlos Aldama at his drum class in San Francisco, 2005. *Courtesy of Chris Walker.*

For years I've been giving a class on Saturday afternoons in San Francisco at Cesar Chavez Elementary School, in the parking lot. It's fifteen dollars for two hours. Usually about ten students show up to learn, but more people come in the summertime when it's warm. They all have professions besides drumming. One is a schoolteacher, another works at the airport, and the other is a lawyer, for example. We study different styles of Cuban music, like rumba and comparsa, but not batá. If I told you that I regularly make more than a thousand dollars a month, I'd be lying. I don't. Sometimes I collect bottles and cans and sell them to recycling. I always pick up loose change when I see it on the streets *por allí*. I use that little bit of money to pay the light bill, the water, or whatever. I'm not ashamed to say it either. It comes in handy. Sometimes that's what I do in order to contribute to the household here. I love my independence and I have my pride.

* * *

Oye, you're interviewing the hell out of me today, man! When do I get paid?! *La muerte alante y la gritería detrás* . . . Do you know what that means? Money first, work after. [laughter] I'm just playing with you. I'm glad you're doing this work, especially as a black person preserving the culture, because it's important that this kind of information come through you. I'm not racist, but it's not the same coming from someone else. And I'm glad to share this with you because I know you are going to take care of it (*sé que tú lo vas a cuidar*).

5

Drum Lesson

* Umi *

I have always been around drums. But I was always more of a dancer. I have always loved languages, of which music is perhaps the most beautiful. But language and dance, although related to the batá, don't make you a drummer. So it has been a challenge to make my hands execute the rhythms I hear so clearly in my head and feel within my body. Sometimes I could play the rhythm but, for lack of technique and strength that come from years of playing, it would be inaudible. I would get frustrated sometimes and my hands would swell as I tried to force sound from the drum. Carlos would say, "If you can't hear yourself, then nobody else can hear you either!" Carlos is seventy years old. But still when he strikes the drum it sounds like thunder, as if the old masters like Pablo Roche and Jesús Pérez are present, playing with him. When the rhythm is just right, he looks into my eyes and lets me know. Then we hold on to the music and stretch it out for a while . . . to really remember.

Carlos struggles to reconstruct in a class setting the habitus, tastes, practices, and modes of bodily expression that went without saying in the barrios of Havana, where his generation learned in the 1940s and 1950s. Some of the musical directives that Carlos gives here might have been obvious in that setting. In the context of our lessons, the instructions are meant for a consecrated drummer who is engaged in active pursuit of esoteric knowledge and who accepts direction with the confidence that understanding and enlightenment will follow initial bewilderment. At intervals throughout all of my lessons with him he would say, "That's

Carlos and Umi studying, 2009. Photo by Sherwood Chen.
Courtesy of Alliance for California Traditional Arts.

good, you're playing correctly, but you need to improve these specific elements in order to really play." He explains what he sees as important techniques that an aspiring batá drummer should master, emphasizing the importance of: *chachá, punta de los dedos, modulación,* and *cruzando.* Later he discusses particular *toques* (rhythms), pointing out how to apply various techniques in the context of actual batá performance, providing relevant background information, and explaining conceptual approaches to each one. Lastly, Carlos offers tips about important miscellaneous points of concern for batá drummers. Even for those not actively involved in studying the drum, this chapter is a window into the process of batá apprenticeship as it takes place.

Carlos explains in chapter 2 how persistence won him entrance into the circle of drummers. He comments throughout this book and especially in this chapter about the difficulties of teaching, learning, and remembering the batá liturgy outside the context of dense communal networks of practice. He repeatedly complains about how there are not enough opportunities to play in the Bay Area. He grounds the lesson by reiterating that *batá is a drum language used together with song and dance.* The process of transmission defies easy comprehension and description. It is tied to the interpersonal and group interactions that occur within master-apprentice relationships, within Añá batteries, and within *toques de santo,* where drum instruction happens. I agree with Hagedorn that what is being taught, after the student learns to imitate the teacher, is how to play *differently* from one's teacher.[1] Carlos calls this creating your own personality. He urges: "Remember, in all these *toques* you can add something . . . You have to own it! Play what you feel." Clearly, to move from mechanical imitation to inspired expression would require serious effort on the part of the student.

Carlos gives very helpful suggestions for aspiring drummers. Pay attention to his advice and try it. This book emphasizes technical suggestions, philosophical approaches to drumming, and explanations of the context and manner in which rhythms are used over notation on the musical staff. Musical notations as found in other texts about batá are valuable.[2] But reading the music alone, removed from any context, does not allow batá to do what they were born to do. We must not forget that batá is an aural/oral tradition that requires intimacy in performance and the process of learning. In order to salute, praise, and summon the oricha with heart there must be competent use of sacred knowledge. If you choose to read through transcriptions by other authors, Carlos's wisdom can help you understand how to use what you have read.

During the time of my studies with Carlos, I also learned from other accomplished drummers and from religious practitioners about the role of the drums. I would ask Carlos his opinion about what they had told me. His reaction was often surprising and/or funny as he agreed or disagreed with them. He was usually careful to say that people do things differently, and that it all depended on what oricha house or drum battery you were from and who had taught you . . . But he was also sometimes brutally honest about how he felt. Through it all, he would say, "Add what I'm going to teach you now to what you already have. That way, your knowledge will be longer . . ."

* *Carlos* *

Some teachers mistreat their students, cursing, etcetera. Pablo used to hit people. He was so good he could play left- and right-handed.[3] He would say to the other drummers, "I'm no machine, I'm not a Victrola, so play right!" But I was never that way. I try to be cooler, converse with you, give you elements to help you understand.[4]

PLAYING FOR THE DANCERS

Another thing, you'll have *santeros* who like to dance. And you have to convince the spirit to come. It's a kind of challenge, with a certain amount of violence to it. You have to open their body to the oricha, split something apart so spirit can enter. With your strength, it becomes a question of how much of this kind of *toque* can you handle, because there is no time to rest. There was a santero who had Ogun made, but he only got possessed when you played *Ochosi Agueré.* Dancing for Ochosi was when Ogun would come. I got tired while playing and I felt like I would die. Everybody was screaming at me, "Don't lose Ogun! *Dále,* Carlos, come on!" You have to be able to hold on, understand? You have to size people up, too. There was one guy who danced to *Meta* Changó and you had to be careful . . . wait a while, *suave* at first, now a bit stronger, a bit more, pull back, push some, catch a second wind, and so on. Know yourself and how much gas you have at any particular moment. Know what you can do, know what you can't do.

Remember that the conversation between the dancer and the drum is very important. You have to *force* the dancer to move, push them. Once you have the basic pattern, you have to add some flavor, a little bit of this, a little of that, so you aren't *pesao* (boring). If you don't change up, dancers get tired of you. In the old days, when a santero or santera came before you to dance, if you didn't have what it took to keep them dancing, they would leave, *pa' la pinga albañiles que se acabó la mezcla* (to hell with it). Today many dancers like to dance fast and hard all the time. Back in the day, it was different. There were real dancers of the batá rhythms. You had to play just what they asked for with their dance steps. This is a give and take – *un toma y dame* – I give and you give back.

Alfredo Olomidara, for example, walked around as he listened to what you were saying with the drum; if he didn't like it he would leave. But when he started to spin it was time for *Alaro* Yemayá, then the *Zapateo,* GANGAN, GANGAN . . . then he might pause, drink a little water, and start again. It's a give and take (*toma y dame*). "Ah, so Umi is a good dancer, huh? He'd better tie his shoes tight to dance to my drum!" And you as the dancer thinking, "So they say Carlos plays well. He's gonna have to play his ass off today!" There was this mutual challenge. You had to conserve your energy!

Nieves Fresneda was one of the founding members of the Conjunto. She was at least sixty years old when the group started and she danced a beautiful Yemayá. Librada Quesada was from the second generation of Conjunto dancers that entered in 1965. She danced a lovely Yemayá solo too, but her specialty was dancing for Eleguá. Nieves, Librada, and most of the other Conjunto performers danced wonderfully on the stage and in real ceremonies. Today nobody really knows how to dance batá anymore. Just Ñongo, Chachalokuafun, and whatever they see every day on television. There are very few today – I'm talking about *in Cuba,* not even the U.S., but *in Cuba* – there are few people who know how to dance batá.

What I want is for you to retain this stuff, any way you can. The batá is a Yoruba dialect, and as such the descendants of the Yoruba understood it. They were enslaved in Cuba, but through oral transmission they learned their dances. And they asked for what they wanted to dance. Since they understood, with their bodies and with song, they requested what they wanted to hear. Today people dance any old way (*bailan lo que les salga de los cojones*), but back then it was different. In that era you played, and if you played badly the dancers would quickly salute the drum and be gone. You would have to sit down and *make* them dance with your playing. Like when people shake the chaworó for Yemayá and Ochun. Some drummer wanted Yemayá to hurry up and come down one day, so he shook the chaworó like mad. "Are you coming or not?" (*¿Vienes o no vienes?*) He had to convince her. It's hard to learn those things anymore, because those old ones died. But I caught a little bit. Taught by Jesús . . .

* * *

When you play you have to dance the drum, you have to move your body. Not dance the same step people are doing in the party, but dance within yourself to what you are playing. As a point of support (*punto de apoyo*). I have always done it like this, I do it this way now, and I will always continue. That way, if ever you make a mistake, you can't get lost because you have the rhythm in your body. *Es un elemento que tienes a tu favor.* (It's another element you have in your favor.) Also, try to play without strapping the drum on. Practice supporting, moving, and controlling the drum without the strap. With *fundamento* yes, strap it on because you can't drop that. But when you're practicing, develop your ability to control the drum.

Just relax, no stress, if you mess up we will go over it again. Don't worry, in the end I'll be more convinced of your ability than you. I'll make sure you know this stuff. When I see you somewhere I'm going to say sit down and play for me. Without self-promotion, *sin autosuficiencia,* I teach what Jesús taught me. Later they'll say, "Umi plays his ass off! Who taught him? Ah, Carlos." What I want is for you to create your own personality through the drum. The youngsters in La Habana today play different, *boom baf boom,* you can't hear the different personalities.

You have to play so that people can't shame you. To do that, you have to learn how to play, and develop your own unique abilities. You have to develop an "antibody" for challenges. Determine and perfect *your* personality. Learn how far you can go, because we're all different. You are younger than me, but I'm *more clever* than you are! Ceremonies are different from dance classes. It's true you studied with me . . . but there comes a time, as you get to know more or less how a toque goes, when you say to yourself, "Let me show Carlos!" But no, show it to Umi! Demonstrate your ability to *yourself.* You have to convince yourself you know this stuff – *Yo soy Umi.* The only way to truly do this is in the confrontation between drummers, singer, and *el público* (the people) at ceremonies. And if I see you out playing I will sing a song to test you. Here in the Bay Area there is not that thick *ambiente* of Santería and batá drums, but in New York there is. I would put you to the test . . . in a minute. I'm a *cabrón* like that. There are so many players who want to be big shots and *tirarse el peo más grande que el culo.* With them I search for the details, and if they don't know, if they aren't clear it shows their weakness and oh well, shame on them!

I sing here in California, but I'm not a singer. I am a drummer. When Galarraga comes from Los Angeles, I drum. Everyone knows me as Carlos *el tambolero.* The real singers are Lázaro Galarraga, Lázaro Pedroso, *cantadores de santo.* There are very few here in the U.S., even in New York. What makes a real singer is a certain ethic. It's your work, it's what you develop and project. You have to search and refine. I'm not the best, but I'm not bad. And what's more, I'll play with anybody. In any kind of challenge I will represent and hold my own (*rendo la ganancia*). My history is there. If I have to sing, I'll take it back to José Antonio el Cojo and all the old heads. In Abakuá I have to sing. And I have to read history to interpret the *diloggun.* I know how to throw diloggun. I know a lot of *oddun.* And I've heard from many old people. Each had his or her own ethic. They had their own unique *tumbao* (way).

THE IMPORTANCE OF THE CHACHÁ

Make your left hand, your chachá, as agile as possible. The strength of your *chachá* opens all kinds of possibilities for your playing – *la medida* (flow), *el nivel* (intensity). You use different sounds (pitches) at different moments. These are small details that you can only grasp with time. You can learn any toque, but there are always details that really make it special. If you want to play you have to be heard. You have to hear yourself. If you can't hear yourself, no one else can either! Competition exists among the drummers, believe me. Somebody is always thinking "I'm better than Umi, and I'm gonna let the world know" ... *Lo voy a poner a guarachar* ... This all exists so you have to be ready. *¡Campanea, cabrón!* (Work your chachá, man!) It's the left hand that leads the right.

THE IMPORTANCE OF PUNTA DE
LOS DEDOS (FINGERTIPS)

If you don't work with *la punta de los dedos* you'll always be early and off time. It's what helps you keep the beat. Without it you'll get lost. If you don't use *tapados* then you are what's called a *mayorcero abierto* (open), and that's not good. The tapado is always going to be an important part of what you're doing. Sometimes it will be more pronounced, sometimes less. It strengthens your chachá. You push the sound out using punta de los dedos. I call this "modulación." You can't hit the drum hard, or the same way, all the time. You have to vary, to give it texture. *Modular* (to modulate). Punta de los dedos allows you to speak Yoruba with the drum. It defines your personality. Don't always play open. There are many toques that repeat what the song is saying. You have to use punta de los dedos. Learn to crawl, walk, then run (*No saltes de gatear a correr*). If you don't practice this, yeah you'll know the toque, but your language won't be clear. What are you saying? Take for example the rhythm *Bariba Ogedema* for Babaluayé. I learned it from Andrés Isaaqui, who improvised on it in different ways that I liked. He used this technique to speak Lucumí with the drum. He would get on my nerves sometimes because he liked to look at my mother's behind, but I loved how he played.

THE IMPORTANCE OF STRIKING WITH BOTH HANDS AT ONCE

La unificación de las manos (the unification of both hands) is very important too, striking both sides of the drum at the exact same time (*cruzar* or to cross). It's what gives you power. So that even when you are tired and have no strength left, you keep the same strong sound. When you play you have to look for the weak points of the santeros to possess them with oricha. You can find that point and exploit it with your chachá and unificación de las manos.

* * *

My intention is not to talk so much of history. My main intention is for you to play the drum. To do that you need to practice; if you don't practice you won't advance.

SPECIFIC RHYTHMS

The toques that go with sung prayers (*rezos*) and certain praise songs (*oriki*) are very specific. Some toques go with very specific songs. They have nothing to do with anything but that. Alubanché for Eleguá is a good example. It's like a phone line directly to him.

[LISTEN TO TRACK 1]

Ewi Pamí is a toque for drummers who know a little Lucumí. *Bara, dide, obara* . . . these words are specific and special to Changó. We play this as a *mojuba* for him. In the old days it was easier to maintain things, to remember the language. Before, drummers used to speak a lot of Lucumí with the drum. This *tambor* does not have a specific ride. Here you are praying, telling an allegory about Changó. So each *mayorcero* will play this one very differently, according to his skill and ability. Pablo Roche, Andrés Isaaqui, and many old-time players in Cuba spoke Lucumí and brought that to the drum. Some, like Jesús, did not actually speak Lucumí, but they had learned the phrasing from Pablo. For example, I don't speak Lucumí, but I play something like what I heard the old ones play. The only part that is fixed is the middle part, the conversation. Ewi Pamí is usually played in the *oro seco* when the toque is for Changó. Afterwards you could play Titilaro, then Meta. Within the course of a *wemilere* you would save this rhythm for special moments: the arrival of a well-known santero, or the presence of some really strong drummers who you wanted to challenge.

[LISTEN TO TRACK 2]

Do you know who invented the toque for that song *Kowo kowo araba yo oriki kowo demi*? It was Armando Sotolongo Blanco. He understood plenty Lucumí; he was an old *tambolero* of Pablo Roche's. At a toque put on by some rich white folks, Andrés Isaaqui played (iyá) and Armando Sotolongo Blanco was on segundo (he was an omo Eleguá who later committed suicide). They started to *sacar majagua* (to woodshed or mess around) because nothing was happening. They invented a new way to play this rhythm because they were bored at the toque! I'll tell you the truth; I never play that. But there is an *aluya* for Changó that is a lot like it. *Sacar majagua* means to practice, to play *for us* (the drummers). Excuse me for talking so much. But you weren't born in Cuba. You didn't grow up among the older generation of drummers in Cuba. So I'm trying to tell you more or less what they told me. Understand? These things I say will serve you. They will. If you don't forget.

Oferere is an *aruya/aluya* (praise) for Changó. We use it to honor him. It is a toque that is very specific to Changó. It is his alone, unlike Iyakotá, Chachalokuafun, and other toques "shared" by various orichas. Here you sing as if you had *cerveza* (beer). You would sing "Ofere awamilodo . . ." People started singing that song with that toque as a sort of short cut (*una facilidad*). In order to excite (*embullar*) the folks at the party, you sing:

Oferere awamilodo awamilodo oferere
Awamilodo Changó awamilodo

"*Hay cerveza,* we have beer." [sings toque] There were two ways to play it: one that was harder with all open tones, which I think comes from the Matanzas style. The other way was easier, with one *abierto* and two *tapados.* You could just as well sing that song over Ñongo. Oferere awamilodo, Gi GI gan . . . What happened was that when it came time to present an iyawó it was easier to sing Oferere instead of *Oba Igbo* (the rezo/prayer), in order to build up the energy of the chorus. People had more fun, and the presentation was nicer, *más lindo.*

Oferere is used to excite the people, to make the iyawó dance, or bring the spirit of Changó through some horse, and to do this with the greatest possible ease. Like in all things, the batá suffered deformations; many old, very traditional songs (*cantos de fundamento*) were lost in favor of more popular, easier songs. At the same time, since there was no formal education in Yoruba-Lucumí language, people answered the akpwon as best they could, from their hearts. And this was accepted. The important thing was the energy.

You could play this if you didn't feel like playing *Titilaro* or *Ewi Pamí,* because no one would dance to those rhythms. Only the oldest santeros knew how to really do it. For example, if some old santero came to the party, you might *moforibale* and pay respect to the person by playing Ewi Pamí. It was also used to insult them.[5] Those who understood would react and say, "I know what you're saying! Don't be insulting me!" But this was lost when Pablo passed.

Bajuba and Meta are toques that you use to work up the spirit. Bajuba, especially, is about praying, *mojubando* (improvising speech, praise) for Changó. You have to watch your energy. Some santeros make you work hard. The ones that get mounted by playing just the drums. Because they're dancers, they love to compete with the drums (*fajarse con los tambores*).[6] Pablo Roche never played Bajuba like his father Andrés Sublime. Jesús never played exactly like Pablo, who taught him, and I cannot play it like Jesús did. Each of us has an emotional, spiritual concept that is different. A different understanding of the batá, even though we are born into the same tradition of respect, love, and consideration. There's always something different between what is yours and what is mine. A distinctiveness between Pablo and Jesús, etcetera. For example, in Meta you can play the opening itótele phrase three times, or as many times as you want, depending on the *mayorcero* and what he likes to hear. It gives the mayorcero the chance to rest. I like to stretch it out. The same iyá call to begin is used to end that conversation.

[LISTEN TO TRACK 29]

Some people play Emi So, which is for Changó, inside of the salute for Obatalá in the oro seco. I never did this and never could understand why some folks play that way. Yeah, there's the road of Obatalá called Ajaguna, the warrior who rides a white horse and wears red and white beads. This is very much related to Changó, but I never could understand why they had to add that part to the Obatalá toque. Jesús did not play it that way either. Other people did. It's valid, but I never liked it. One time at Pepa's oricha house in Regla when Jesús was learning itótele under Pablo Roche, a drummer named Quintín embarrassed Jesús during Emi So. Pablo got Jesús up and sat with Quintín himself, like in defense of his student. Later on he got on Jesús's case real bad and made sure he learned this *toque* correctly.

Titilaro is an especially difficult rhythm for Changó. As the iyá player you have to really lead. Nobody can tell you where the beat is. It's up to you. But it is counter time (*contratiempo*). You have to sing the *tambor*. If you don't play every day you'll forget, unless you can sing it. You can play it different ways, but always with the same rhythmic concept. That way you'll know for sure you're playing it right. That's how I've always played it. You have Titilaro on tape. Now listen to it, study, but don't get flustered (*no desesperarte*). Experience will allow you to understand a little more in the future. You have to dance it and sing it, *ya tú sabes.*

Agayú is a rhythm for the oricha Agayú, which has its own special little details. If you don't play them it just isn't right. They are subtle and hard to explain.[7] Agayú is imagined as a volcano. He cannot be as agile, for example, as Changó or Ochun. Agayú has to be very strong and rough (*rústico*), stiff and almost clumsy. In the last section of Agayú, the off-time feel is especially important. The itótele player has to hold on tight in order to not get thrown off. Everything has to sound forced, heavy, slightly out of time. *Punta de los dedos* is key here. A nice mound of *fardela*[8] on the iyá helps develop that chop. Jesús used a lot of fardela, because he had huge hands. You have to play this basic ride for those who really know how to dance for Agayú. That's what they are gonna want to dance to.

[LISTEN TO TRACK 19]

Elekotó goes directly with a certain song for Agayú. There was an old tambolero named Andrés Isaaqui who never learned to play Elekotó correctly. If you started to sing this he would say, "*¡Voy a mentar madre!*" (I'm going to curse you out!) As the mayorcero you have complete freedom to improvise, but when the *akpwon* calls *Elekotó to de o,* you MUST respond with the correct call, no matter what improvisation you're doing at the time. Like a phone call you gotta answer: *Me llamaron. ¿Quién es?*

[LISTEN TO TRACK 3]

Bonko Iwonlo is a specific toque for Obatalá. What I call a *tambor de élite* (exclusive rhythm). It's like singing Emi Alado for Changó. You wouldn't start here necessarily. You might start with *Oricha Pawa Pawa Pawa Oricha.* But most of these songs you never hear around here. When

I sing I have to hold back from singing many of the most beautiful songs, because no one knows them. At the same time this is hurting me because I forget.

Yansan is one of the most specific toques for Oyá. We play it in the oro seco. On the last part of the toque the intensity increases (*va en ascenso*). But take your time (*dáte tu tiempo*). When you play *mayor* (iyá) you are in control. Okónkolo and itótele are following you. Don't run all the roads together, one after the other. No. Make the division between each road clear. You have to control the tendency to rush through it. Each road has its own level. All these nuances (*cositas*) you have to keep in mind. If not, your speech won't be clear. And people will ask, "What is he playing?" Identify the *distinct moments* within each toque. Feel secure about what you know how to play. You have to dominate the drum. You have to! If you don't, people will not respond to your drumming.

[LISTEN TO TRACK 24]

You could play this rhythm with the song Ayiloda ya okuo, but it's you *contra el canto*, you have to be on beat. You could use Twi Twi. These aren't easy toques. You have to sing them. Certain toques are especially tough. Chachalokuafun, Ñongo, Iyesá, and so on, are simple, but there are batá toques, like this one, that are real ball busters (*roncan la pinga*)! I never tell my students that what you're playing is bullshit. If you learned a different way from someone else, fine. Now let's study some more. I'll show you how I learned, and that's that. Ku ta TA TA – Ran. The chachá is the signature part of that rhythm.

Twi Twi is another toque for Oyá. It's been years since I played these conversations that go with it. *¿Pa' qué engañarte?* (Why try to fool you?) It's not like I played this yesterday. Before I spoke pretty good English, but since I haven't been practicing it's slipped. It's the same way with this toque. But we're going to work it out as cleanly as possible. *Cada toque tiene su propia musicalidad* (Each rhythm has its own musicality). As much as you want to add to spice it up is valid.

Alaro is *the* signature toque for Yemayá, the one we play in the *oro seco*. Inside of it you can *mojubar* for Eleguá, Ogun, Changó, Obatalá.

These are elements in your favor. You use the same *llames* (calls) for other toques . . . then you fall back into Alaro. [sings examples: Eleguá, Ogun, etc.] You have to practice and find *la medida*. People will say, "What an Alaro Umi played!" You can't do that in every toque, like Obatalá (oro) or San Lázaro. You can do it in *Meta,* as long as you are playing slowly. Everyone doesn't do it. It depends on your teacher and the concept he has given you. You have to have mental agility to play around with the boundaries of the traditional toque.

[LISTEN TO TRACK 26]

The beginning of this toque, the slow part, is especially a question of creativity. It all depends on the moment. It's not the same playing Alaro for the oro seco as playing it to call the oricha during a ceremony. Understand? It's the same toque but different intensity levels (*niveles*). Sometimes in Alaro, if you're playing for a santero that is *muy subidor,* you can start with the last road *para ahorar un poco* (save some energy). Later, if you want, you can go back. This is a trick, a strategy. The *Zapateo* for Yemayá can be played early in Alaro; it doesn't have to be at the end as most players do it now. The end would just taper off. I don't know why, but this is how it used to be played. I guess everything is subject to change.

Omolode is a rhythm we play for Yemayá. But really it's for Ochosi. Okay? [sings]

Ochosi awalode omoricha awalode
Ochosi omomi bawa o omoricha awalode

Omolode omotitiyo eleyolade

Orubanchikini Orumbatolokun
Eran kimbe oni yan ya o Olofi olomi ode

Omo chikini
Ara modanse

Ibara Ochosi omomi ibara
Ochosi omomi

This started to be sung for Yemayá through Conjunto Folklórico Nacional. We would sing it for Ochosi, but Yemayá took it over (*se la cogió*). So many children of Yemayá get possessed with that song. But it is for Ochosi-Odede. Everybody sings it for Yemayá now, but really it's for Ochosi: Emi ode omo ode, omo ode emi ode *Tú y yo, yo y tú.* You are me, and I am you. That's what this song means. The end of the rhythm is called the Zapateo:

Omo chikini
Ara modanse

Sokutaniwo is another toque mostly for Yemayá, but also sometimes for Changó. Don't worry about the adornments. Learn the base first. Later the adornments are what you create. Here you have to use punta de los dedos even more. You have to play at a certain level. The drummer has to adapt to the singer and vice versa. A good singer will push you, and you have to push back. Let your hands be free so you can really play. Don't hold on to the drum, *suéltalo* (let it go).

Cheche Kururú is the most specific rhythm for Ochun. On *rezos* or prayer rhythms like this you get to *rubatear.* This means to stretch and play with the *clave.* You can take your time; go as fast or as slow as you want. The true song for this *toque* is Yeye Oro Ye o . . . Ye Ye . . . Cheche Kururú . . . Kowaniye.

[LISTEN TO TRACK 25]

Cheke Ochun is an elite toque within the liturgy. These are specific toques for specific oricha. This one is for Ochun and you cannot sing it for Obatalá or Changó or any other oricha. There used to be people who knew how to dance to these rhythms. There's a big difference between the first generations of blacks born in Cuba and the youth of today. As the old ones passed on, the younger ones came along, they forgot a little and added a little . . . Cuban style. That's how we have the Lucumí language that is used in Santería ceremonies and everyday Cuban speech today. This should be sung and played when Ochun possesses someone. It's an allegory about her. Even though Ochun is the youngest of the oricha, she is given respect as an elder because only she was able to reach Olofi and save humanity.

Next comes *Tosun Tosun Chatumarete. Yeye Milodo mo chatumarete,* which means, "May your body and soul rise like smoke." These are toques where you must really focus on pronouncing language with the drum.

Eni Obobo Soloju is another *tambor de élite.* It has to do with women's menstruation. Like Foma Okete or Bajuba it is very specific. The story is a kind of puya or even punishment. One of Ochosi's wives (Ochun) was fascinated by the fact that the animals he brought home from the hunt never had any blood. She got so curious that she decided to investigate. It was that Ochosi (Odede) offered the blood to Olofi, that's why they had no blood. Ochun opened a small hole in the sac where Ochosi carried his animals and she put flour there, so she could follow his path. No one was supposed to see this; it was secret. So when Ochun found the place where Ochosi and Olofi would meet, Olofi realized her intrusion and punished her. Since she wanted to see blood, she would see blood. From then on she would have a menstrual period. When children of Ochun dance this rhythm, they cover their genitalia and act as if they feel pain there.

[LISTEN TO TRACK 4]

SHARED RHYTHMS

Ñongo and Chachalokuafun are rhythms that were adapted to batá from other drum traditions besides the straight Yoruba that were brought to Cuba. Arará and Iyesá were adapted this way too. The old ones said, "Let's make a toque that can be used with *cantos de bembé.*" For example, you were Iyesá and you came to my house, I am Yoruba. I want you to enjoy yourself, so I come up with a batá rhythm that can accept your Iyesá songs. These are toques that various oricha share in common. You can sing for many oricha with these same rhythms: Iyakotá, Yewa, *Rezo* (prayer) or *Hueso* (bone), Iyesá, Ñongo, Arará, etcetera. Like I said before, other batá rhythms are much more specific.

First you used to mark everything in Ñongo, but then Pablo Roche said to hell with it and played the new thing. Same with Chachalokuafun, which means "something that cuts." It used to go one way, but then Pablo changed it.⁹ Apart from maintaining the tradition with a certain level of strictness, he did innovate things. The adornments in Ñongo and Chachalokuafun come from what you feel. When people are dancing and singing, full of the spirit, that's when these rhythms get hot and changes happen. It's definitely a give and take. It's not anything I can really teach you. The rivalry between the singer Lázaro Galarraga and me pushed toques like Ñongo to great heights. He would say, "I'm gonna bust your hands," and he really would! The energy we created would make the drum sweet.

[LISTEN TO TRACKS 5 AND 6]

ADVICE FOR AÑÁ DRUMMERS

When playing itótele, don't expect to go back to the beginning of a toque, or follow any set pattern. Listen to what the mayorcero is going to do. You have to be right with him. Here in the U.S., you can't afford to adapt to the way one person plays like I adapted to Jesús. There just aren't enough opportunities to play like that. So you have to play with everyone. You put together your style by taking bits and pieces from other drummers. You include that in your repertory along with what you feel. These are what somebody called "blue notes," these inspirations that you get, and that are hard to repeat. Something you received, something your heart created in the moment. If you recorded it you might be able to do it again, but not with the same feeling.

It's very important to relax as you play, and to strike with your hands, not with your body or your facial expression. I mean it's not a question of moving your head or lips to play the drum. Don't think that the uglier the face you make, the better or stronger you'll play. It doesn't work that way. But a lot of people seem to think so. The agility has to be *in your hands*. If you don't relax and dance when you play *güiro*, you'll be hurt up (*te vas a despingar*). It's true. The *chequeré* is one of the toughest instruments to play, especially for a long time. If you don't dance, you're through. Let your body go, dance it (*báilalo*)! It's a clash between the instrument and your body to see who wins.

Sometimes drummers pee blood. First of all, it's caused by bad positioning and posture. You're straining too much. It can happen anywhere, ceremony or dance class. It's one of the most important things you must learn: how to sit and set up comfortably, in order to avoid too much strain. Also, make sure to drink plenty of water to wash out your kidneys. This will help too. I rarely pee blood when I play because I know my limits. It only happens if somebody, like a good singer, really pushes me, or maybe if I have too much fun or get angry.

Don't tape up your hands (*no te pongas padrapo*). It only makes your hands moist. You can lose the pigment in your skin, it can get infected, etcetera. In Cuba we called it *siete cueros* (seven skins). This happened to Jesús Pérez. He started using tape and his fingernail got infected. He ended up using a thimble on his finger when he played.

A drummer should abstain from sex the day before a tambor de fundamento. He should sleep clean (*dormir limpio*). The singer is free – the songs are sacred but there's no contact with any sacred object like the drum, which is an oricha itself. The few occasions when I've played sucio it's been because there was no choice. I ask forgiveness from Añá. I do a cleaning. But I always avoid at all costs playing dirty, because this goes against you . . . against your body, against your religious beliefs. Some people do this because they are shameless (*por descaro*), you know, they don't care and to make a little money they'll play *sucio* without a second thought. But those who practice a strict regimen about this, they respect these rules. *El sudor de la mujer se te queda.* (A woman's sweat stays on you.)

* * *

There's going to be a *tambor aberikulá* (party with unconsecrated batá) on July 3. I'd like you to go, so you can sit and play. I'd like to see what you can do. Okay? This doesn't mean I would sit you down at a *tambor de fundamento.* Maybe at some point, but I would have to determine that after seeing you play. I want to see what you've practiced, there with the people and with Lázaro Galarraga, who is a good singer.

Speak . . . just like you speak English. Don't rush to come in. Take your time. You have to take a small breath. It's that small space where you have to come in. With all these toques remember you can add something to it. You got it! Why? Because you are Umi! You have it, so you have to own it! Play what you feel (*lo que tú entiendas*). You have it in your legs. For the simple reason that you have brains. "Watch this, motherfucker!" (*¡Tú verás ahora, cabrón!*) is what you have to say. Then do your thing!

6

The Future, What Comes Next?

* Umi *

From Havana, the batá tradition has spread around the world, especially to Puerto Rico, Miami, New York, and California. Scholars discuss the important contributions of key drummers from Cuba who established batá drumming in the United States. Cuban expatriate drummer Julio Collazo is credited with introducing the batá drums to the United States, although he did not teach the tradition to others until very late.[1] Collazo was born in Havana in 1931, where he began to play batá in his early teens.[2] He later joined the well-known drummer Nicolás Angarica, and after this early experience, he became a protégé of Pablo Roche and traveled with him throughout Cuba to play religious/ritual ceremonies. In the 1940s, Katherine Dunham, African American choreographer and anthropologist, hired Collazo to tour the world with her performance company. After leaving her group, he worked as a popular musician in New York City, where he played mostly for Latin jazz and dance music recording sessions with the likes of Mongo Santamaría, Tito Puente, Eddie Palmieri, and others.[3] Only occasionally did he play for religious ceremonies. In 1961, Collazo led the drumming in the first ever batá ceremony on U.S. soil, and in 1976 he led the first U.S. ceremony to use consecrated batá.[4] He is said to have taken on a small number of students in the 1960s, to whom he taught basic batá techniques. In 1975, he built a batá set of his own. At the time of Friedman's study, "those who currently play batá in New York . . . learned from Julio Collazo or one of his students."[5]

Collazo and Orlando "Puntilla" Ríos are mentioned among key figures in New York. Ríos was born in Havana in 1947 and died in New
York City in 2008. He came to the United States with the Mariel boat
exodus in 1980 and became known as a master batá and rumba drummer. He founded the important folkloric group Nueva Generación (New
Generation) and became a major influence for batá drummers in the
United States. He worked closely with the Caribbean Cultural Center
in New York.

Other Cuban *bataleros* who spread the tradition include Onelio Scull
in Puerto Rico, Pedro "El Negro" Rayat in Miami, as well as Alfredo
"Coyude" Vidaux and Francisco Aguabella in California, especially Los
Angeles. Aguabella was born in Matanzas sometime around 1925. He
started playing rumba and other folkloric music in his home region.
Later, in the 1950s, he moved to the United States, where he worked as
a percussionist in Cuban and Latin jazz groups. (Like Julio Collazo,
Aguabella's U.S. debut was with Katherine Dunham.) He did a lot of
important work teaching and performing Cuban music in Los Angeles, where he lived for many years until his death in 2010.[6] Non-Cubans
like John Amira (white American), Milton Cardona (Puerto Rican),
and Eugene "Gene" Golden (African American) in New York; (African
Americans) Yagbe Gerrard, Marcus Gordon, Otobaji Ngoma, as well as
Peter de Jesús (Puerto Rican American, aka Piri Ochun), and Michael
Spiro (white American) in California played important roles in spread-
ing the batá drum tradition. Jazz musician Bill Summers has worked
to extend the tradition in California and the South, especially in New
Orleans.[7]

Since the publication of Yoruba practitioner John Mason's seminal
work *Orin Orisa* on Yoruba chants in the diaspora, with its in-depth
tracing of batá drum tradition from Cuba to the United States, other
consecrated sets of batá or *fundamento* have come to the United States
under Cuban and non-Cuban ownership, and more African American
drummers have emerged who are skilled enough to deserve the appel-
lation of *kpuatakí* (master/teacher). Bill Summers brought a set from
Matanzas called Añá Agueré, consecrated by Estéban "Chachá" Bacallao. I am aware of at least six sets of *fundamento* that have arrived in the
San Francisco Bay Area since Mason's work: Michael Spiro brought the

drums Añá Lade Odo Meji Ará Okó from Matanzas and Oke Bi Añá from Havana; José Francisco Barroso (Cuban) brought the drum Añá Lade (Añá Has a Crown) from Havana to the Bay Area; Eric Barberia brought another set from Havana called Añá Ilú (The Town's Drum); Carlos Mena (Dominican American) brought a set from Matanzas called Añá Abolá (Añá Brings Me Prosperity); and African American drummer Otobaji Ngoma created a set in Oakland called Iwori Jiwowo. David Frazier (an African American aka David Flavor) has emerged as a highly respected lead drummer for Santería ceremonies and an important teacher for apprentices to the drum. In addition to playing, Rick Ananda (Indonesian American) is an accomplished batá "mechanic," who prepares and repairs drums with great skill. California is one of the places outside of Cuba where the Afro-Cuban batá tradition is most deeply rooted.

A process is constantly underway in which a new generation of musicians replaces an older generation; a new generation is called upon to continue a cultural core of tradition; and simultaneously or from time to time, a new generation naturally innovates within the musico-cultural tradition. Travel to Cuba, travel from Cuba and the immigrant experience, mixed parentage, and master/apprentice relationships between regional groups all play a part as well. The fact that one of the masters of ritual batá drumming moved to the Bay Area of California is very significant in the history of the drum and its continuing evolution. Children like one named Ode Bi, born to a father from Matanzas and a mother from Oakland, taught by African American and Cuban masters (including Carlos Aldama) is a perfect example of what is to come. *Añá unsoro!!!* The drum speaks.

* Carlos *

I don't like people to call me *maestro*. The best title to me is Carlos Aldama, the drummer – *el tambolero*. The fact that I had enough dedication to learn the drum, and that I had so many positive experiences along this path has been a blessing. *Una bendición*. Not everyone in Cuba was this lucky. There were a lot of guys from my era who never learned much about the drum, even though they played with Jesús Pérez and other greats. Even still, they didn't learn. Some learned from Jesús, but so what? They never became one with the drum. There have always been drummers that play hard and strong. But the best drummers play with *una ética* (an ethic) and with style. What I am trying to do is *transmit* to you all that I've learned and experienced as a drummer. Every new generation should keep in mind the roots. But remember to create your own style. You can play what I play, but you won't feel what I feel. So you have to express *your* feelings, your perspective. Find yourself within the drum. It won't happen overnight; it takes a while. Time is king.

RETURN TO CUBA

I went to Cuba just recently because I needed to see my family, and so that my two American goddaughters, Pamela and Carolina, could meet their religious family in Cuba. I was sad to find out that Jesús's son traded the house at Soledad 415 between San Rafael and San Miguel (*hizo una permuta*). He's a successful doctor, but to me this was a bad decision. He didn't analyze the situation well. He didn't consider how important that house was in the history of the drum. Many important drummers passed through there. Right in front of the entrance is where many of the well-known photos of Jesús's funeral were taken. It was a sacred kind of space. But Jesús's son didn't understand – or maybe he did and didn't care. The place was an apartment in a solar. Jesús had built a *barbacoa* to get the most use out of the space, but it wasn't enough room for the three of them: Jesús's son, his wife, and their child. Maybe his lack of concern was because he had nothing to do with drums. He said he wanted to see me on this trip, but I didn't have time. I was on the way to the airport when he called.

* * *

During my visit, I walked around almost like a foreigner, looking at the drummers, and taking in everything. I felt disoriented. It seemed like such a long time since I had been in Havana. My goddaughters and I had to get the hang of riding in the *carros particulares*,[8] because they don't stop anymore! They really don't. You have to just jump in! I was like a country boy in Havana (*estaba como un guajiro en La Habana*). Looking here, looking there, always surprised by what I would see.

On the first day I arrived we went to a bembé for Babaluayé/San Lázaro that a godchild of my ex-wife Santa's was giving. I dropped my bag and hit the street, and I didn't come back until five in the morning. I went to my old neighborhood, the solar where I used to live. I woke people up. "Mira Carlos!" they would say. Then I went over to the Barrio chino because I was hungry. I made it back home, slept for a while, woke up, and went to the bembé. Yvette really wanted to go to a batá ceremony; that's all she talked about. We went to one that started about seven o'clock at night in Cayo Hueso. I went in, *pan,* and one guy shouted "Mira Carlos! That's Carlos, everybody!" And people were like, "So you're Carlos Aldama." And I said, "Yes, I am."

Next I went to see my daughter, Dalia, for her ocha birthday. On the way someone heard batá drums playing. At this point I was tired because we'd only been there three days and it felt like I hadn't sat down. "They're playing around here somewhere!" And sure enough we walked around a little and found the toque. At first I stood outside and watched through a window. Later I recognized someone and went in to say hello, and as I did a young man came up and spoke to me. He was the son of one of Jesús Pérez's godchildren. He grew up in the house where Jesús made ochas, and where we did Jesús's last rites (*Las Honras*). He recognized me as "Michel's father," not as Carlos. It turns out that he owns the drums that were playing. Yvette wanted to stay, but I was hungry. I greeted all the young drummers, the new generation, and then I left.

In all I went to about three tambores: one for San Lázaro that they put on for a Mexican guy, a few blocks from my house, another in San Leopoldo, and one more. I was asked to play a few times but I didn't. I let the youngsters have it. For the most part no one remembered or recognized me at the drumming ceremonies in Cuba. The youth don't remember anyone (*la juventud no se acuerda de nadie*). Or maybe they do, a little, but the problem is the following: no one has taught them the old stories, the consciousness, the legacy of the old-guard drummers. Understand?

And the ones who would know were at home resting (*estaban sentados en sus casas*). People like Papo Angarica, Mario Aspirina, and so on.

The rhythms were the same in the oricha parties. But each generation has its own swing. Each generation has its moment. Right now belongs to them. When I started, the older drummers were there and then the youth arrived – my cohort. I'm from the second or third wave of drummers, from Pablo Roche on down (*de Pablo pa' ca*). Understand? The old heads recognized me then, so now I have to do the same. The music is still beautiful to me.

OBSERVATIONS IN HAVANA

To tell you the truth, I didn't venture out much during my visit. Besides a couple of trips to the cemetery to place flowers on my parents' and on Jesús's tombstones, I stayed in Cayo Hueso. I was more interested in being around my family and in my neighborhood. Maybe if I'd had a rental car I would have gotten around more to visit people. But to catch any kind of transportation – whether a car or a bus – was more than a notion. To get to the cemetery in Vedado was even tough. Just imagine how hard it was to reach Guanabacoa (*imagínate tú Guanabacoa*). To get there we had to do a lot of talking and pay extra money. It wasn't easy. We would wait two or three hours for buses. I wanted to go to a lot of places, to see folks like Bolaños, go to my Abakuá lodge, and so on. But I didn't do a lot of that because of the transportation problem.

The buildings were falling down. But people still had the same character about them. There are still a lot of beautiful women in Cuba too! [laughter] Yvette would playfully hit me, because I was looking at the women. But even she had to admit. And it wasn't even summertime. One taxi cab driver said, "That's the only thing Communism hasn't been able to take away, the fine ladies!"

The youngsters were not interested in politics or anything like that. They were all about enjoying their lives, their moment, and their youth. Why? Because now's their time. By the same token, like anywhere in the world, poor people are suffering. Yvette would notice a decaying building and ask, "No one lives there, right?" When I told her that people do live there, she would cry. Down by the Malecón, for example, there was a big house and a small store where you could buy beer and food for *chavitos* (the equivalent of dollars); right next to it was a pitiful house, almost falling down. Yvette and the girls wondered why this hadn't been fixed too. I explained that in some cases the government puts priority on construction that will have immediate economic rewards. Maybe the folks who used to live in the place that's all fixed up have been moved to an apartment outside the city, or maybe to a hostel somewhere. That's when the government puts the business in their place, to make some money for the country.

Paladares don't exist anymore. There were twenty-four pesos for each *chavito*/dollar. A lot of people were waiting at the dock, hoping to jump on some vessel to reach the U.S. They would jump in the water and swim to the thing. The young people were *luchando,* robbing, assaulting folks. Police were constantly asking for young people's ID (*carnet de identidad*). My grandson doesn't like to go around with his ID. He says it's a drag (*es pesao, cae mal*). One day I sent him out to do an errand for me and he got picked up by the police and taken to the station, because he didn't have his *carnet.*

Yvette and I were there for twenty-five days. Carolina and Pamela were there for ten days. At Christmas time we kept the same old tradition of eating roasted pork, drinking rum and beer with family. People drank a lot to try to forget about their problems.

RECORDING BATÁ IN CALIFORNIA

This is an example of what batá was like in my era in Cuba. I really enjoyed the recording session at Cal State Monterey Bay. It felt good playing with you, Rick, Calvin, and Taji. I made some mistakes and my playing was a little off sometimes (*no estaba actualizado*). But I was able to cover it up because we played with my own drums, which I know well. Very few drummers from my generation have had the chance to leave a record like this. I am one of the few of the old guard left, so this recording is an important legacy. It might seem crazy, but for me the most important thing about it was this mark on my knee. I used to always have this dark spot, almost like a callus or birthmark, from the weight of the

Carlos Aldama with Bay Area batá drummers, 2010. *Beginning second from left,* Mikhail Lebrada, Carlos Aldama, Umi Vaughan, Lázaro Galarraga, Yagbe Gerrard, David Frazier, and Piri Ochun. *Photo by the author.*

drum. It had disappeared, but it came back (*se revivió*) from playing so hard for this recording. This was a great satisfaction! A simple and very wonderful thing.

FIESTA DE CHANGÓ

On July seventeenth there was a big *tambor* for Changó at my house in San Leandro (California). My goddaughter gave the party in honor of my wife Yvette's Changó, because Yvette is her *oyugbona*. In La Regla de Ocha you have to put on a drumming for both of your godparents' oricha before you can play in honor of your own. You have to acknowledge your elders first. The party was really good. And I live for parties like that, especially at my own house. Some say it was the *tambor del año,* the party of the year. Even people who couldn't come have called me on the phone talking about it. Lázaro Galarraga, who is a santero and one of the greatest singers from Cuba, was here. Sergio Obangoché came through. Most all of the representative santeros in the Bay Area were at the tambor. Piri Ochun's fundamento drums were playing.

It's a shame that Piri is leaving the area *(¡Me cago en diez que se va!).* But I've always known him to be a spirit in motion. So it's no surprise to me. I know I will see him again. Yvette cried a lot, but I didn't get too upset. Now that Piri is gone there could be less toques here in the Bay Area. The other fundamento drums don't play much, mostly because there are more *fundamento* here than there are *santeros!* Plus everybody has to work so much and so hard. In fact, you are more likely to see batá drummers at a cultural center or a dance class than at a *tambor.*

TOQUE FINAL

Everything I have I owe to Añá, to the drum – homes, trips, everything. I'm not rich. But through the drum I support myself. When I feel like drinking a beer or some rum, I can do that. The real richness, though, is seeing my students become part of my drum lineage. The best reward is seeing my hard work, and that of many before me, expressed in my students' playing. My hope is that through projects like this book, and in their very lives, my students will carry on the batá tradition.

If I were in Cuba, I would probably be sitting at home, not doing much, and this is not appealing to me. That's what has happened with many musicians of my generation. They don't want to argue with, convince, or prove themselves to the younger generation. The old Africans *(negros de nación)* used to say, *"La última me la llevo para la sepultura."* (The last bit I'll take to my grave.) This means that they purposefully refused to share all of their knowledge; there was always something left out, not taught. I think it was a mistake. But they did so based on their experience in Cuba, because their culture was devalued.

Many times the next generations, the *criollos* and *reyollos,* were not interested in learning and maintaining the culture. So the old ones said, "If you are not going to care for this knowledge, then I will keep it." Many older musicians agree, but I think this is a mistake. I try to be open as

Carlos Aldama at the door of Jesús Pérez's old house in Havana, Cuba, 2008. *Courtesy of Carlos Aldama. Photo by Yvette Aldama.*

long as I know that the student is serious. If they don't have good intentions, then I won't take them on. I'll teach those who deserve it. But not just any and everybody. There are many who play batá and I pay them no attention, because they don't love it. They see it like a slave master sees slaves, as an object. I've had the chance in my life to observe this. They could be nice people, but they will never *really* have it.

Slavery ended in Cuba in 1886, but I am a slave to the drum. I have dedicated myself totally. That's why my name will live on. Physically the old drummers are no more; but they are here spiritually when we play batá. We die and move on, but the drum stays. (*Yo me voy, pero el tambor se queda.*) If I had not become a drummer I don't know what would have become of me. It's destiny, right? Whether you become a *desgraciado* or a decent person, rich or poor, is a question of destiny. Me, I live and die with the drum. But I don't plan to die yet. As long as I can move even an eye I'll keep playing, because this is my life.

You have to get more into the batá drumming scene. You have to be at the toques and *claim your place.* I know that you're modest and unassuming by nature. But you have to assert yourself (*imponerte*). When a student graduates and leaves the university, he or she must study all over again. Because the things you encounter in the real world are totally different. In order to reach your destiny, you have to go deeper. It's a special commitment you have to make. A journey into your self and into the drum.

* * *

To close the wemilere we play the rhythmic salutes to eggun and the oricha Oyá, Babaluayé, Osain, Yewa, and Yemayá. While we play and sing there's a bucket of water sitting in front of the drums. After that a santera, usually a child of Yemayá, dances the bucket in circles to the Alaro rhythm. Sometimes as an *ebbó* the host of the ceremony will throw three coins into the bucket of water, and maybe a little *chekete.* (But it's not necessary.) Nowadays some people put more money in. The money is not for the person dancing the bucket. It's just an ebbó, symbolic. When she's danced the bucket out into street, dumped it, and returned to the drum, then the last songs are sung for Eleguá and Olokun. *E ago Elegua e . . . Ago Elegua . . . Olokun bawa o Bawa orisa awa o e . . . Bobo aita ekue leko e . . . Olokun ewe de.* This last one is only for tambores de fundamento. Last, we play a short phrase on the drum to end it all. *Ache to ache bo ariku bawa dede wantolokun to iban echu.*[9]

CONCLUSION

The Drum Speaks Again

Ga dum, ga dum, dum . . .
And we rode the rhythms as one, from Nigeria to Mississippi, and back . . .

Etheridge Knight (from the poem "Oba Ilu, The Talking Drum")

We began this book with the understanding that the batá drum is a vessel, a vehicle, and a teaching tool. The drum holds on to various kinds of information, including sonic patterns, stories, family and ritual lineages, herbal medicine, and magic. It keeps the beat to and through which humans live. At times we "imitate and repeat the timeless acts of the oricha, approaching and aligning [our]selves with the real world of aché."[1] At other times, drum beats salute various members of the community and acknowledge their various identities and relationships to one another as servants of this or that oricha. Sometimes the drums invite and incite trance possession, becoming "cables upon which man cross[es] that chasm" between the profane and the spirit worlds. To play is to "force open the door to the source."[2]

Carlos's stories about his birth, the help of midwives who used African herbs and techniques, and the origins of his grandparents in Yorubaland, demonstrate strong ties to Africa. His discussion of his father's side of the family and the legacy of the Spaniard Domingo Aldama point to *mestizaje* (race mixing). In this process of cultural and genetic blending, there was force – in the form of rape, relationships of control and convenience – and feeling, expressed through genuine love and concern between both parties. His grandmother's pregnancy by Aldama suggests one, and Aldama's establishing her in a home outside of Havana suggests the other. Carlos's stories about his grandmother's initiation as an oricha priestess also reveal shifts in Yoruba ritual practice in Cuba. In Yorubaland, priests and entire towns are often devoted to one oricha. In Cuba, each priest serves several main oricha, even though they are especially dedicated to one. Carlos's grandmother was initiated in Matanzas according to old African style and received one or two oricha to care for, while Carlos, like most in Cuba, received several.

Carlos's stories also illuminate the social position of Afro-Cubans who played batá during his epoch. They were almost never "professionals": doctors, lawyers, politicians, and so on. On the contrary, they were most often close to or fully immersed in the informal economy of their time. Pablo Roche was a moneylender. The lady who kept Jesús Pérez's schedule was also a cook for neighborhood prostitutes. Jesús Pérez and Trinidad Torregosa seem to have been exceptions, the former being a carpenter and the latter a chauffeur. This kind of class distinction seems to have been more pronounced for drummers than oricha priests. Carlos refused to teach his instructor's son batá because it was "preferable" for him to become a surgeon. There were more middle-class priests than there were middle-class *tamboleros*. Today, at least in the California Bay Area, this situation is reversed; privileged people have access to the drum and the time to study it, not to mention travel to Cuba. I am a university professor and artist in addition to being a batá drummer.

In this book, Carlos Aldama clarifies, gives image and voice to little-known yet important people, events, and beliefs: the Yemayá procession in Regla, opinions about spirit possession, homosexuality, and friendship. Carlos helps to explain why and how some of Cuba's most famous drummers achieved their status. His words round out and give color to the lists of drummers and drum lineages. For those who wonder why it is important to mention the names and deeds of so many dancers, singers, and drummers: this book is a kind of *mojuba,* an honoring of those who came before us and paved the way.

This book will help anyone who wants to better understand the batá tradition and the apprenticeship by which one becomes a drummer. Do not think, though, that by reading these words you have made the journey. Like Carlos says, "I am not going to make you into a drummer. *You are!*"

DRUM SONG

In his well-known book *Santería,* Joseph Murphy is self-reflective about his role as a white anthropologist/practitioner telling the story of an Afro-Cuban religion. He questions what right he has to be there and especially to speak, based on his outsider status. Finally he determines that by recognizing Santería as a product of the suffering of African peoples in the New World and a monument to their creativity and resilience, he earns the right to *represent,* albeit from a position of limited knowledge and authority. He points also to the fact that Santería addresses universal human values and emotions – thus granting him access by his very humanity. I agree with Murphy. I also concur with anthropologist Elizabeth McAlister and historian Bernice Johnson Reagan that it is important for communities to tell their stories and document their traditions *for themselves* whenever possible.[3] I say that, since Cubans in the United States aren't studying, African Americans need to be the ones to learn, practice, and *own* the batá drum tradition. Own in the sense of: to fully inhabit, be responsible for, to honorably control. For these reasons Carlos and I feel a certain poetic justice and power in our study together.

In his poem "Oba Ilu, The Talking Drum," Etheridge Knight describes a group with representatives from Africa and the Americas, threatened by a heavy, menacing "deadness." This "stillness [is] unlike the silence after lovemaking, or the pulsating quietness of a summer night." Instead it is "skinny, brittle, and wrinkled." I interpret this stillness as the end of drum song summoned by black hands. It is one of the many dangerous, possible outcomes in transcultural war. Knight also evokes the unity of diasporic communities – "the heart beats, blood flows slowly" between them. By poem's end, the drum conquers the stillness: "And the day opened to the sound . . . Ga dum, ga dum, dum . . . And we rode the rhythms as one from Nigeria to Mississippi and back."

Carlos Aldama emphasizes that the main purpose of the drum is to build unity and community. Three drums speak as one, calling together all the various members of the "village." He stresses the importance of feeling. Batá is not mechanical. On the contrary, for Carlos, his ability to play is tied to moments, images, scents, and experiences with other drummers, dancers, and singers. This is the half that has not been and cannot be told, because it must be *lived*.

MOTHER TONGUE

I always wanted to learn an African language. When my sister and I would travel as youngsters, people would often curiously ask us where we were from. Presumably because of our dark skin and facial features we seemed exotic, definitely not American. We would always take this opportunity to break into some invented "African" brogue, which confused or satisfied our questioner and more importantly indulged our own desire to know Africa, especially through the intimacy of language (thought and expression). This journey with Carlos – both learning the language of the drum and helping to tell his story, woven of Afro-Cuban Spanish – has been truly amazing. In my work, I am pursuing the drum, home, and myself. Home being Africa. Admittedly, this is no geographical Africa, accessible by plane. It is a mythical, symbolic Africa that for many of us in the diaspora really means honoring and serving our ancestors, knowing and loving our origins and ourselves. This Africa materializes for me when I play batá. Fittingly, for those committed to one day soon uplifting our home communities scattered like satellites around the world and to redeeming the mother continent, encountering the Africa within may be a prerequisite to effectively engaging the real Mother Africa.

Carlos and I had the chance to play together at a festival for Ochun put on by the music-dance collective called Emese, Messengers of the African Diaspora. It happened at the Malonga Casquelourd Center for the Arts in Oakland, in a large, sun-filled dance studio.[4] The first thing I noticed was that there were a lot of children. Wide-eyed toddlers played with the bells on the iyá drum and chased each other about. (My son, Rumi, would have been right there with these miniature *bataleros,* but he stayed home that morning.) Older kids glided over the wooden floor with blinking tennis shoes on wheels. In the corner there was an altar on which cool water, rum, a cigar, Hawaiian flower necklaces, and coconuts awaited the community ancestors. There were photographs of three important artists who died over the last several years: musician and organizer Johnette Coleman, dancer and teacher Carlos Aceituno, and percussionist Bernard Wray.

At the focal point of the room, there was an exquisite throne of golden fabric, sunflowers and roses, oranges, *caramelos,* and money for Ochun. All the light from the windows and mirrors danced in the colors around the altar. Beautiful women wore smiles and flowing white cloth with flashes of yellow. Men with slick hats and crisp shirts congregated around the drums. It was Sunday morning and people looked like they were going to church, African Diaspora style. There were Cubans, including *santeros* and heavyweight drummers like *matancero* Sandy Pérez, and even Carlos Aldama with his wife Yvette. There were folks from Barbados, Trinidad, Puerto Rico, black southerners, Mexicans, Asians and Asian Americans, as well as some whites. Oakland was in the house. And since it was Ochun's day there were special guests from Oshogbo, Ochun's hometown in Nigeria.

The festival got underway with libations and greetings. We sang a few eggun songs and even a Palo song because Baba Bernard used to love that. Some folks wept but there was more joy than sadness. Two teenage girls danced *hula* for their late grandmother Johnette, whose photograph looked on from the shrine. There was to be a community dance class with Cuban and Nigerian style Yoruba music/dance. The whole first half of the class we did straight Cuban rhythms beginning with Cheche Kururú nice and slow. One of the Oshogbo guys brought a Nigerian batá and played it while the African Americans played Cuban batá. Some of the drummers were thrown off by his improvisations at first, but it sounded perfect to me. The groove was sweet. People closed their eyes and seemed to smile within, swaying like the river. The atmosphere thickened. After a while I changed to the song *Yeye bi o bi Osun ooo,* which requires the *toque* called Iyakotá. Later I switched to the song *Ide were were ide Ochun* and our crew of African American (and two Asian American) drummers naturally switched to Dadá. Carlos emerged from the crowd of onlookers and stood beside the drums. He was giving us a look like "C'mon, guys! Let's go!" He wanted to hear our drummers speak more freely and forcefully. With his insistence they finally did.

Then the Nigerians took over. First they taught a song that invites everybody to move gracefully like Ochun. Next, they showed us a *toque* on the Cuban batá that fit with several other beautiful songs they were

singing. Then they began to dance and the energy multiplied. I was playing itótele, feeling great. Calvin was on iyá and James on okónkolo. In
the beginning, we had been just holding on trying not to lose the new
rhythm, but now we could hear it and began to loosen up and really
play. A young woman, a priestess of Ochun who recently moved to the
Bay Area from Matanzas, was nodding her head and singing along. At
this point, I noticed Carlos taking off his rings getting ready to jump in.
He told Calvin to let him have a little bit and sat down. Carlos got into
the groove effortlessly and swept us all – the drummers, singers, and
dancers – deep into the moment. He slapped, cracked, and rumbled so
magnificently with the Nigerian rhythm that time stopped. Sweat flew
and a collective smile/cry stretched throughout the Malonga Center:
Ochun Yeyeo!!!! I looked around and some people's eyes said that they ap-
preciated the diaspora "magic" of this moment with African Americans,
Cubans, and Nigerians honoring Ochun and creating Yoruba music together. Everybody else was simply exalted, enjoying for other reasons.

After the dancing, folks embraced and basked in the heat we had created. Meanwhile we drummers played a salute for the eggun before the
altar. Later we shared technical advice, encouragement, and fist bumps.
A man in a wheelchair with a flash of *collares* (ritual beads) around his
neck sipped on orange-infused mint water. Girlfriends laughed, posing
for pictures with Ochun and her throne. Eventually, reluctantly, people
did leave. The warm August afternoon was calling and there were activities everywhere in the city. But the effects of the Ochun festival were not
totally fleeting. As people departed, they took with them fruit and flowers, vivid images and rhythmic memories, and most importantly they
took away *positive energy.* This we all can use to heal the (social) wounds
and keep on making a way in this mad, wonderful world.

FUTURE RESEARCH

Much work remains to be done in tracing Yoruba culture from Africa to
the New World and deciphering its multiple, altered meanings in new
homes. There is a great need for a Spanish translation of John Mason's
seminal book *Orin Orisa.* Beyond this there are thousands more songs
from the Santería musical liturgy that need transcription and translation
into the various languages of the African Diaspora, especially English

and Spanish (the main languages of most Santería practitioners). Also deserving of study are the reasons why African Americans, especially youth, rarely embrace batá drumming even within African American oricha communities. As tied as we are to music and the drum (think hip-hop, R&B, etc.), and as spiritual as we are (the black church), it is a wonder why knowledge of and excitement about batá is limited among African American young people who have been exposed to it. This understanding could go a long way in fomenting a new generation of *bataleros* among African American youth.

Another area for study is the role of dance classes as sacred spaces, especially in locations outside of Cuba (like the California Bay Area), where *toques de santo* happen infrequently. It seems that since there are fewer ritual gatherings, people bring that same spiritual energy to oricha dance classes, which are the next closest thing. Batá drummers who otherwise have limited opportunities to practice and maintain their "chops" come to the classes and play their hearts out. Like Rara processions in Haiti and New York or Second Line marches in New Orleans, here singers, dancers, and drummers periodically infuse their communities with the healing energies of African Diaspora performance.[5] The result is an experience that blurs the line between "folkloric dance class" on one hand and "real *wemilere*" on the other.

It also remains to explore the lives of other "walking Rosetta Stones" like Carlos Aldama. Their lives are truly windows into an era that will soon be lost entirely. They are treasure troves of information and tradition.

MODUPE

Thank you to the ancestors, to Eleguá, Ochun, Obba, Changó, and all the oricha. Peace to Mother Africa. Love and Respect to the entire African Diaspora. ¡Viva Cuba! Maferefun Añá. Long Live the Drum. Aché!

[LISTEN TO TRACK 30]

Umi Vaughan

Carlos Aldama and Umi Vaughan, The Drum Speaks, 2008.
Photo by the author.

GLOSSARY

aberikulá unconsecrated batá drums

aché the power to make things happen

aguardiente fire water, strong alcohol

ahínamá common colloquial expression, meaning "it's just right, keep it right there"

akpwon lead singer in a Santería ceremony

aleyo non-initiate in Santería

aluya an honor or homage, a special toque rhythm for oricha especially when used to create high energy and induce trance possession (e.g., Meta for Changó or Twi Twi for Oyá)

amalá ritual dish of cornmeal porridge prepared for Changó

Añá the spirit of the drum, the spirit of sound, very closely associated with the batá drums and the oricha Changó

ángel de la guarda guardian angel, main oricha that "owns" a person's head

arayé argument, discord, negative energy

asere colloquial for buddy, friend, derived from "I salute you" in the language of the Abakuá secret society

babalawo high priest in the Yoruba tradition, diviner par excellence

banté cloth apron used to adorn the batá drums for sacred ceremonies

batá trio of hourglass-shaped, double-headed talking drums of the Yoruba people preserved in Cuba

batalero batá drummer

bembé a music party celebrating the oricha

bonkó Afro-Cuban word meaning friend, or brother

brujería literally witchcraft, used as a synonym for all Afro-Cuban religious practice (sometimes, but not always, pejorative)

cabrón rascal

canto a song for the oricha

carro particular taxi that goes up and down main thoroughfares in Havana, usually old-model American cars

chachá the smaller head of the batá drum

chancletica small leather strap used to play batá in Matanzas, Cuba

Changó Yoruba deity of thunder, lightning, dance, drum, and male virility

chapista auto body repair person

chavito slang term for Cuban "convertible pesos" equivalent to the U.S. dollar

chaworó necklace of bells placed on both sides of the lead drum (**iyá**) of the batá ensemble, used to attract positive energy and keep away evil spirits

clave rhythmic pattern that guides most Afro-Cuban music

collares color-coded bead necklaces that represent the various Yoruba oricha

comparsa neighborhood-based music groups that perform in carnival processions; another name for the **conga** rhythm that they play

conga procession rhythm and happening from eastern Cuba (especially Guantánamo and Santiago)

coño an exclamation, "Damn!"

criollo/a black Cuban born of parents brought directly from Africa (africanos de nación)

dar coco literally "to give coconut," a Lucumí divination ritual with coconut

derecho money earned for any service within the context of Afro-Cuban religion or music

ebbó sacrifice in Yoruba tradition

ecobio brother, fellow member of an Abakuá lodge

efun white powder used in Lucumí (Yoruba) religious practice

eggun ancestor

ekelekuá an Afro-Cuban version of "oopsy daisy" or "there we go"

Eleguá Yoruba oricha of the crossroads, decisions, all languages, insatiable appetites

empeó judge (**la ley**), a role or position within the Abakuá society

enú the larger head of the batá drum

fardela a brownish, wax-like paste applied to the larger head of the iyá (and sometimes itótele) to adjust the pitch

fundamento refers to consecrated batá drums, or anything regarding Santería that is considered to have deep roots

golpe drum lick or phrase

guagua bus

guajiro country person, farmer

guapería gangster behavior

guaposo tough guy, gangster

güiro a beaded gourd instrument (aka chequeré); also a style of music/ensemble that is used to celebrate the oricha instead of batá

Ibaé Tonú Rest in Peace

invento a creation or invention that adds on to an established way of playing

itá divination ceremony held on the third day of the seven-day-long Santería initiation ritual called kariocha

itótele middle drum of the batá ensemble

iyá largest and lead drum of the batá ensemble

iyawó new initiate into Santería, literally "wife" of the oricha

Iyesá refers to a Yoruba subgroup brought in large numbers from West Africa to Cuba, and to specific drums and drum rhythms they use on the island

juego Abakuá lodge

juramento swearing in, initiation as a ritual drummer

kpuatakí master batá drummer and teacher

llame a call played by the lead drum (iyá) to initiate specific rhythmic sequences (toques)

Lucumí said to have been a greeting among enslaved Yoruba during colonial times, it refers to Yoruba-descended people and culture (religion, language, music, food, etc.) in Cuba

madrina godmother, initiator into the religion of Santería

maferefun Yoruba for "Give praise to . . ." used to express thankfulness or reverence to the oricha

Malecón Havana's oceanfront promenade

mambí Cuban soldier in the Cuban Independence War of 1895

mayorcero iyá player, lead batá drummer

medida the flow of a particular rhythm

mestizaje race mixing

Meta the number three in Yoruba, name for a special rhythm for oricha Changó

modupe Yoruba for thank you, I appreciate . . .

moforibale literally "I scrape my head on the ground" (I prostrate myself), traditional Yoruba greeting used to show respect to elders

mojubar verb meaning to pray and praise, both verbally and/or with the drum, from Yoruba "mo juba" (I give honor)

mokongo the leader or head man of an Abakuá lodge

nivel the intensity of a particular batá rhythm

obá ritual leader for Santería ceremonies

Obatalá Yoruba deity, eldest of all oricha

Obba Yoruba river deity, wife of Changó

Ochosi Yoruba deity of the hunt and police force

Ochun Yoruba river deity, wife of Changó

oddun a figure in Yoruba divination (whether Ifá or diloggun)

Ogun Yoruba deity of iron, the forge, medicine, and war

okónkolo smallest drum and time keeper of the batá ensemble

Olodumare almighty creator god of the Yoruba (along with Olofin and Olorun)

omo Añá ritual batá drummer, literally son (omo) of the spirit of sound

oricha cultural hero, venerated ancestor, or force of nature

oro cantado liturgy sung outside the altar room (after the oro seco) to the accompaniment of batá as part of Santería music celebrations to salute all major oricha

oro seco drum liturgy played inside the altar room as part of Santería music celebrations (wemilere, toque de santo) to salute all major oricha

ossogbo negative energy

oyugbona secondary initiator into the religion of Santería, literally "eyes on the road," he/she carries out instructions of the primary initiating priest (padrino/madrina)

padrino godfather, initiator into the religion of Santería

paladar restaurant run out of a home, serving typical Cuban cuisine (comida criolla)

palero practitioner of Congo religious rites in Cuba

Palo Congo-derived religious tradition maintained in Cuba

pato homosexual man

pesao a jerk, unpleasant person, boring

plante a semi-public Abakuá ceremony that incorporates drumming, dance, and song

posada a place, similar to a hotel, where Cubans rent rooms for amorous encounters

potencia Abakuá lodge

puya literally thorn, songs or batá rhythms used to goad the oricha into "mounting" initiates in trance possession

quinto highest pitch drum in the rumba ensemble (tumbadora=lowest, conga=middle)

Regla de Ocha literally law of the oricha, synonymous with Santería

repiqueteo improvisation on the batá drum

reyollo black Cuban whose grandparents came directly from Africa (de nación), and whose parents were the first generation born in Cuba (criollo)

rubatear to intentionally alter or play with the melodic line and timing of a song

sacar majagua among batá drummers, to "woodshed" or practice

Santería Afro-Cuban religion based mostly on Yoruba beliefs (from what is now Nigeria) with some Catholic borrowings (e.g., Yoruba oricha paired with Christian saints/santos)

santero/a practitioner of Santería

solar lower-class housing, tenement building with shared patio

Suama an African language preserved in Abakuá societies in Cuba (especially Matanzas)

subidor a person who embodies, or becomes "possessed" by, the oricha

tambor drum, also individual batá rhythm, and the ceremonial party that uses batá music

tambolero batá drummer

tapado a muffed tone on the batá drum (itótele and iyá), often pronounced *tapao*

toque a batá rhythm, and a ceremonial *gathering* with batá music

toque de santo religious party usually incorporating batá drums

tortillera a lesbian

traje special ceremonial outfit worn on only a few ritual occasions in the life of the initiated Santería practitioner, color coordinated to represent certain oricha

warriors Eleguá, Ogun, Ochosi, three important oricha of the Yoruba pantheon worshipped in Cuba

wemilere a Yoruba-Lucumí religious party with drumming

yambokí serious apprentice to the batá drum tradition

ya tú sabes a Spanish phrase meaning "You already know . . ."

NOTES

Introduction

1. Rogozinski, *Brief History of the Ca-*
ribbean, 8.

2. Chomsky et al., *Cuba Reader;* Clus-
ter and Hernández, *History of Havana;*
Scarpaci et al., *Havana;* Kapcia, *Havana;*
Rogozinski, *Brief History of the Caribbean.*

3. Miguel Barnet, *La fuente viva*, 183.

4. The Yoruba cultural area covered
Nigeria and the east of Benin, as far as the
kingdom of Ketu. The Arará were from
the kingdom of Allada, in the south of Dahomey, near the slaving port of Ouidah.
The Bantu (Congo in Cuba) inhabited the
south of Cameroon, Gabon, the Congo
(formerly Congo-Brazaville), Burundi,
Rwanda, Congo-Zaire, and Angola, as far
as the north of Namibia. Calabar (source
of Carabalí [Abakuá] culture in Cuba)
stretched between Nigeria and Cameroon, from the coast to Lake Chad. See
Roy, *Cuban Music*, 12; see also Brandon,
Santeria from Africa to the New World.

5. Martínez, *The Open Wound*, 42.

6. C. Moore, *Castro, the Blacks, and
Africa*, 102.

7. Knight, *Slave Society in Cuba;*
Pérez, Jr., *Cuba Between Empires;* Scarpaci
et al., *Havana*, 3.

8. Barnet, *La fuente viva*, 265.

9. Deuteronomy 28:25.

10. Gilroy, *The Black Atlantic*, 205.

11. hooks, "In Our Glory," 47.

12. Gilroy, *The Black Atlantic*, 195.

13. Patterson and Kelley, "Unfinished
Migrations," 15. See also Butler, "Defining
Diaspora."

14. Johnson, *Diaspora Conversions*,
37–38.

15. Ortiz, *La Africanía;* Gilroy, *The
Black Atlantic;* Béhague, *Music and Black
Ethnicity;* Daniel, *Dancing Wisdom;*
Nwankwo and Diouf, *Rhythms of the Afro-
Atlantic World;* Vaughan, *Rebel Dance,
Renegade Stance.*

16. Klein, *Yorùbá Bàtá,* 21; Atanda, *Introduction to Yoruba.*

17. Klein, *Yorùbá Bàtá,* 13.

18. Usually in Spanish *oricha* (without
any *s*'s) is used for both singular and plu-
ral: for example, *los oricha.*

19. Cabrera, *Yemayá y Ochún,* iii.

20. Amira and Cornelius note the
dominance of the Havana tradition in
New York City (*Music of Santería,* 15). In
Santiago de Cuba, *fundamento* drums
born from both Havana and Matanzas are
used, but the Havana performance style
is dominant. Sometimes the styles are
mixed, with the Havana style maintaining
prominence.

21. Behar, *Translated Woman,* 12.

22. See Vaughan, *Rebel Dance,* for the
results of my research on contemporary
Afro-Cuban music.

23. In the Abakuá tradition, masked dancers called *ireme* perform precise foot patterns that they use to symbolically trace sacred diagrams on the ground. In addition to the costumed *ireme*, regular members of Abakuá, like Carlos, perform the dance as well. See Miller, *Voice of the Leopard.*

24. Grele, *Envelopes of Sound.*

25. Vélez, *Drumming for the Gods*, xviii.

26. Clifford and Marcus, *Writing Culture*, 106, quoted in Vélez, *Drumming for the Gods.*

27. Vélez, *Drumming for the Gods*, xviii.

28. Cluster and Hernández, *History of Havana*, 50.

29. Cabrera, *Anagó*; Santiesteban, *El habla popular cubana de hoy.* See also Cabrera's *Cuentos negros de Cuba, El Monte, Yemayá y Ochún*, and Lachatañeré's *¡¡¡Oh, mío Yemayá!!!* (1938) for examples of "retelling" Afro-Cuban stories.

30. Behar, *Translated Woman*, 12.

1. Fundamento

1. Bascom, *Yoruba of Southwestern Nigeria*, 13–15.

2. Falola and Childs, *Yoruba Diaspora*, 4.

3. Brandon, *Santeria from Africa to the New World*, 55; see also Matory, "English Professors of Brazil," 72–103.

4. Brandon, *Santeria from Africa to the New World*, 56.

5. Brown, *Santería Enthroned*, 68–69.

6. Bastide, *African Civilizations*, 10.

7. Murphy, *Santería*, 33.

8. Matory, *Sex and the Empire*; Tishken et al., *Şàngó in Africa.*

9. Yoruba descendants in Cuba pronounce this as *oricha*, influenced by the Spanish language, which does not have the ş/sh sound of Nigerian Yoruba or English.

10. Edwards and Mason, *Black Gods*, 3–4.

11. For more information about each oricha, see also Bascom, *Yoruba of Southwestern Nigeria*; Edwards and Mason, *Black Gods*; Mason, *Orin Orisa.*

12. Mason, *Orin Orisa*, 8.

13. Klein, *Yorùbá Bàtá*, 189. See also Benkomo, "Crafting the Sacred Batá Drums"; Lovejoy, "Drums of Şàngó."

14. Vélez, *Drumming for the Gods*, 50.

15. Mason, *Orin Orisa*, 54.

16. Mason, *Orin Orisa.*

17. Moreno, "Festive Rituals"; Ortiz, *Los cabildos*, 6.

18. Roy, *Cuban Music*, 13.

19. Bastide, *African Civilizations*, 95.

20. Brandon, *Santeria from Africa to the New World*, 70–71.

21. Brown, *Santería Enthroned*, 66.

22. Mason, *Orin Orisa*, 9.

23. Brown, *Santería Enthroned*, 70.

24. Ortiz, *Los cabildos*, 14.

25. For descriptions of the ritual initiation process see Mason, *Orin Orisa*, 21–32; Hagedorn, *Divine Utterances*, 212–19; and M. Mason, *Living Santería*, 4–9, 57–83.

26. Hurston, *Tell My Horse*, 221.

27. Hagedorn, *Divine Utterances*, 117.

28. Ibid., 118.

29. The famous batá drummer Trinidad Torregosa was called *E meta lokan* – you are three in one. Clearly this is a Lucumí translation of his name, which means "Trinity" in Spanish, but it could also be said of the batá drums. Mason, *Orin Orisa*, 18.

30. The *enú* is the larger head of the batá drum. The *chachá* is the smaller head.

31. Ocha is a contraction of oricha.

32. For more on women batá drummers, see Hagedorn, *Divine Utterances*, 89–97; Pryor, "House of Añá"; and Sayre, "Cuban Batá Drumming and Women Musicians."

33. This image of "jalando santo," or pulling down the oricha, is found also in Brazil, where Yoruba-derived communities speak of "puxando" (pulling) in refer-

ence to the task of the soloist whenever call-and-response singing is concerned, whether samba, Candomblé, or so on.

34. Estéban Vega Bacallao aka "Chachá" (1925–2007, Matanzas) is considered to have been one of the best batá drummers in twentieth-century Cuba. He learned from highly respected drummers like Carlos Alfonso and Miguel Alcina (Vélez, *Drumming for the Gods*, 58).

35. The Matanzas Abakuá lodge that Carlos speaks of was the "grandfather" of his own lodge in Havana. The seniority of Matanzas relative to Havana in Abakuá is similar to Cuba/United States in terms of the transition of the batá drum tradition.

36. John Mason understands this nuance as the difference between *omo oricha*, or *oloricha* (child or caretaker of the oricha) versus *babaloricha* or *iyaloricha* (mother/father of the oricha), understood as mature/elder priest (personal communication).

2. Learning My Trade

1. Ortiz, *Los tambores*; Mason, *Orin Orisa*, 13.

2. Brandon, *Santeria from Africa to the New World*; Marcuzzi, *Historical Study*; Brown, *Santería Enthroned*, 63–65.

3. Orovio, *Diccionario de la música cubana*, 387.

4. Many Santería practitioners warn that this formula can also result in "the blind leading the blind" (especially outside of Cuba), when untutored communities accept and perpetuate questionable practices.

5. De la Fuente, *A Nation for All*, 335.

6. R. Moore, *Nationalizing Blackness*, 3–4.

7. Ibid., 2.

8. Hagedorn, *Divine Utterances*, 196–97.

9. See also Miller, "Jesús Perez."

10. R. Moore, *Music & Revolution*, 200.

11. R. Moore, *Nationalizing Blackness*; de la Fuente, *A Nation for All*.

12. Domingo de Aldama (in 1836) was among the most prominent slave importers, deeply invested in Matanzas plantations, twelfth richest on the whole island of Cuba. The grandiose structure of Palacio Aldama exemplifies the huge profits of illicit slave trading. After becoming a cigar factory in the 1880s, it is currently home to the Cuban Institute of History (Cluster and Hernández, *History of Havana*, 77).

13. Others have interpreted Pablo Roche's nickname *Akilakpa* as "Arms of Gold."

14. Rogelio Martínez Furé is a folklorist, born in Matanzas, Cuba, in 1937. He worked in the Instituto de Etnología y Folklore de la Academia de Ciencias de Cuba, focusing on the influence of African cultures in the Americas. In 1962, he founded the Conjunto Folklórico Nacional, with which he traveled the world (Orovio, *Diccionario de la música cubana*, 285–86).

15. A *solar* is a tenement building with a shared patio.

16. *Ecobio* means "brother" in the Abakuá secret society, and by extension, "friend" in colloquial Cuban Spanish (Santiesteban, *El habla popular cubana de hoy*, 159).

17. Trinidad Torregosa was a drummer from Havana, Cuba (1893–1977). He was known as a skilled singer and drum maker. He worked closely with Cuban ethnologist Fernando Ortiz and other researchers interested in the African elements of Cuban music. He traveled to Haiti, Dominican Republic, and the United States. He appeared on audio recordings and in films. He was also a member of the Conjunto Folklórico Nacional (Orovio, *Diccionario de la música cubana*, 479–80).

18. Nicolás Angarica authored an important text about the rituals of Cuban Santería entitled *Manual de Oriaté* (ca. 1955).

19. *Asere* is colloquial Cuban Spanish for "buddy" or "friend." It derived from "I salute you" in the language of the Abakuá secret society (Santiesteban, *El habla popular cubana de hoy*, 48–49).

20. Mason (*Orin Orisa*) says the co-conut and candle offering represents kola nut and palm oil, gifts of respect and greeting in Yorubaland.

21. In my own experience in Havana, some batá batteries played Ibaloke for iyawós consecrated to male oricha and Alaro for those consecrated to female oricha.

22. Pancho Quinto (Francisco Mora) passed away in Havana in 2005.

3. Batá in the Revolution

1. R. Moore, *Music & Revolution*, 222.

2. Hagedorn, *Divine Utterances*, 115–16.

3. R. Moore, *Music & Revolution*, 212–13.

4. Benkomo, "Crafting the Sacred Batá Drums," 143.

5. Vélez, *Drumming for the Gods*, 90.

6. C. Moore, *Castro, the Blacks, and Africa*; R. Moore, *Music & Revolution*; Hagedorn, *Divine Utterances*.

7. R. Moore, *Music & Revolution*, 186.

8. Ibid., 187.

9. Hagedorn, *Divine Utterances*, 117; Bettleheim, *Cuban Festivals*, 137–69; Yvonne Daniel, "The Economic Vitamins of Cuba: Sacred and Other Dance Performance," in Nwankwo and Diouf, *Rhythms of the Afro-Atlantic World*, 19–40.

10. Hagedorn, *Divine Utterances*, 110.

11. Vaughan, "Shades of Race in Contemporary Cuba."

12. Mason, *Ironti Aponni Meji*; Rolando, *Forever Present, Oggun*.

13. De la Fuente, *A Nation for All*, 337.

14. Mesa-Lago, *Economy of Socialist Cuba*, 197.

15. C. Moore, *Castro, the Blacks, and Africa*; Hagedorn, *Divine Utterances*, 197.

16. R. Moore, *Music & Revolution*, 214.

17. Ibid., 196.

18. Ibid., 229.

19. See R. Moore, *Music & Revolution* (187–88) and Hagedorn, *Divine Utterances* (143–68) for the perspectives of María Teresa Linares and others involved in this incident.

20. Each person's experience is different. Many years after the situations Carlos describes, María Teresa Linares was instrumental in helping me (U.V.), a black man, attain a position as an apprentice researcher at the Fundación Fernando Ortiz in Havana.

21. Lázaro Ros was a well-known Yoruba singer (1925–2005). He made recordings in Cuba and for the collection Chante au Monde in Paris. He traveled the world with Cuba's Conjunto Folklórico Nacional (Orovio, *Diccionario de la música cubana*, 423; see also Mason, *Ironti Aponni*).

22. Carlos used the term "*cultura*" in reference to the state apparatus that regulates the arts in Cuba. I chose to translate Carlos differently here to avoid confusion, because afterwards he speaks of culture (also *cultura* in Spanish) in the more common sense of "shared beliefs and practices."

23. Santería practitioner and scholar Miguel Ramos identifies Adofó as Alejandro Alfonso (*Empire Beats On*, 155).

24. Mercedita Valdés was a singer of folklore and popular music from Havana (1928–96). She traveled and performed abroad with composer Ernesto Lecuona and also with a show called Zun-zún Babaé. She performed Afro-Cuban music regularly on Sunday afternoon radio programs on the station Radio Cadena Suaritos. She gave performance-demonstra-

tions at academic conferences organized by Fernando Ortiz (Orovio, *Diccionario de la música cubana*, 493).

25. In 1967, the National Council for Culture (which later becomes Ministry) founded Orquesta de Música Moderna under the direction of saxophonist Armando Romeu. This group spawned musicians that later joined or founded other bands of great importance in the development of Cuban popular music. In 1973, pianist Chucho Valdés leaves Orquesta de Música Moderna to create the pioneer group Irakere. Irakere (which means "forest" in Yoruba) incorporated Afro-Cuban religious instruments (batá drums, chequeré, agogó, etc.) until then used only in ceremonies, or on occasion in a few cabaret shows or academic demonstrations.

26. Sergio Vitier is a guitarist and composer born in Havana in 1948. He performed regularly with the National Symphonic Orchestra. He composed music for Cuban films, including: *Girón, El Programa del Moncada, De cierta manera*, and *La Tierra y el cielo* (Orovio, *Diccionario de la música cubana*, 505–506).

27. Spaniard Joaquín Rodrigo composed Concierto de Aranjuez in 1939.

28. Founded in the late 1960s, Grupo de Experimentación Sonora was inspired in large part by the musical movement called Tropicalismo, led by stars like Chico Buarque, Gilberto Gil, and Caetano Veloso in Brazil (Sarusky, *Grupo de Experimentación*, 65). GES also made avant-garde soundtracks for new Cuban films of the time, incorporating various styles and technologies into their recordings.

29. "FolkCuba" was a multifaceted dance, drum, and song workshop presented by Conjunto Folklórico Nacional de Cuba beginning in 1986. It was for non-Cubans only and aimed at attracting tourism.

4. Diaspora

1. Mason, *Orin Orisa*, 3.

2. Daniel, *Dancing Wisdom*, 51–52.

3. For more on Jesús Pérez's role in opening the batá to new audiences and players, see Miller, "Jesús Perez."

5. Drum Lesson

1. Hagedorn, *Divine Utterances*, 131.

2. For notations of batá rhythms, see Amira and Cornelius, *Music of Santería*; Courlander, *Treasury of Afro-American Folklore*; Ortiz, *Los tambores batá*; Summers et al., *Batá Rhythms from Matanzas*; Scweitzer, *Afro-Cuban Drum Aesthetics*.

3. In figure 2.1, Pablo Roche sets up to play left-handed. In figure 2.2 he sets up to play right-handed.

4. Wilson, *The Drummer's Path*.

5. Mason (*Orin Orisa*) translates Ewi Pamí as "the disheartened turtle" and classes it as a *puya* or goading rhythm.

6. Carlos often uses fight imagery, *despingar* (to fuck up, or literally to castrate) in describing the drums' role in inviting spirit possession.

7. In regard to the subtleties of the drum, batá master David Frazier once said, "It's impossible to explain, but you know what I mean."

8. *Fardela* is a brownish, wax-like substance always applied to the larger head of the iyá and sometimes the itótele to adjust the pitch.

9. Carlos says that in Pablo Roche's day, before the 1950s, the lead parts for Ñongo and Chachalokuafun were played as in the beginning of tracks 5 and 6, respectively; and that Pablo invented the styles that most players use today, as from the middle to the end of tracks 5 and 6. Can you hear the difference?

6. The Future, What Comes Next?

1. Friedman, *Making an Abstract World Concrete*, 107.

2. Julio Collazo was born in Havana in 1925, according to Orovio's *Diccionario de la música cubana,* 114.

3. Ibid.

4. Mason, *Orin Orisa,* 19.

5. Friedman, *Making an Abstract World Concrete,* 107–108.

6. Orovio, *Diccionario de la música cubana,* 20. See also the documentary film, *Sworn to the Drum: A Tribute to Francisco Aguabella,* by Les Blank.

7. Friedman, *Making an Abstract World Concrete;* Vélez, *Drumming for the Gods;* Mason, *Orin Orisa;* Summers, *Studies in Batá.*

8. *Carros particulares* are taxi cabs that travel up and down main thoroughfares in Havana, usually old-model American cars.

9. *Con Dios comenzamos y con Dios terminamos.* We begin and end with God.

Conclusion

1. Murphy, *Santería,* 133–34.

2. Deren, *Divine Horsemen,* 249.

3. McAlister, *Rara!,* 20.

4. Malonga Casquelourd (1948–2003) was born in Douala, Cameroon, but began dancing when his family moved to the Congo. He moved to New York in 1972, and then relocated to California in 1976, where he became a very important dance instructor and mentor. He founded the dance troupe Fua Dia Kongo. Tragically, Casquelourd was struck by a drunk driver's car and killed; the former Alice Arts Center was then renamed in his honor. *Dance on in the afterlife, Malonga!*

5. McAlister, *Rara!,* 3–4; Turner, *Jazz Religion,* 45.

REFERENCES

Amira, John, and Steven Cornelius. 1999. *The Music of Santería: Traditional Rhythms of the Batá Drums.* Reno, Nev.: White Cliffs Media.

Angarica, Nicolás Valentin. 1955. *Manual de Oriaté, religión Lucumí.* Cuba.

Atanda, J. A. 1980. *An Introduction to Yoruba History.* Ìbàdàn, Nigeria: Ìbàdàn University Press.

Barnet, Miguel. 1981. *La fuente viva.* Havana: Editorial Letras Cubanas.

Barnet, Miguel, and Estéban Montejo. 1994 [1968]. *Biography of a Runaway Slave.* Willimantic, Conn.: Curbstone Press.

Bascom, William. 1984 [1969]. *The Yoruba of Southwestern Nigeria.* Long Grove, Ill.: Waveland Press.

Bastide, Roger. 1972. *African Civilizations in the New World.* New York: Harper & Row.

Béhague, George H. (Editor). 1994. *Music and Black Ethnicity: The Caribbean and South America.* Miami: North-South Center, University of Miami.

Behar, Ruth. 1993. *Translated Woman: Crossing the Border with Esperanza's Story.* Boston: Beacon Press.

Behar, Ruth, and Lucia Suarez (Editors). 2008. *The Portable Island: Cubans at Home in Diaspora.* New York: Palgrave Macmillan.

Benkomo, Juan. 2000. "Crafting the Sacred Batá Drums." In *Afro-Cuban Voices on Race and Identity in Contemporary Cuba,* ed. Pedro Pérez Sarduy and Jean Stubbs. 140–46. Gainesville: University of Florida Press.

Bettleheim, Judith (Editor). 1993. *Cuban Festivals: An Annotated Anthology.* New York: Garland Publishing.

Blank, Les. 1997. *Sworn to the Drum: A Tribute to Francisco Aguabella.* Documentary film. Flower Films.

Brandon, George. 1997. *Santeria from Africa to the New World: The Dead Sell Memories.* Bloomington: Indiana University Press.

Brown, David. 2003. *Santería Enthroned: Art, Ritual, and Innovation in an Afro-Cuban Religion.* Chicago: University of Chicago Press.

Butler, Kim D. 2001. "Defining Diaspora, Refining a Discourse." In *Diaspora,* 10.2 (Fall 2001), 189–219.

Cabrera, Lydia. 1996a [1954]. *El Monte.* Havana: Editorial SI-MAR S.A.

———. 1996b [1974]. *Yemayá y Ochún: Kariocha, Iyalorichas y Olorichas.* Miami: Ediciones Universal.

———. 1993 [1940]. *Cuentos negros de Cuba.* Miami: Ediciones Universal.

———. 1970. *Anagó, vocabulario lucumí: el yoruba que se habla en Cuba.* Miami: Colección de Chihorekú.

Chomsky, Aviva, Barry Carr, and Pamela María Smorkaloff (Editors). 2004. *The Cuba Reader*. Durham, N.C.: Duke University Press.

Clifford, James, and George Marcus. 1986. *Writing Culture: The Poetics and Politics of Ethnography*. Berkeley: University of California Press.

Cluster, Dick, and Rafael Hernández. 2006. *The History of Havana*. New York: Palgrave Macmillan.

Courlander, Harold. 1996 [1976]. *Treasury of Afro-American Folklore: The Oral Literature, Traditions, Recollections, Legends, Tales, Songs, Religious Beliefs, Customs, Sayings, and Humor of People of African Descent in the Americas*. New York: Avalon Publishing Group.

Daniel, Yvonne. 2005. *Dancing Wisdom: Embodied Knowledge in Haitian Vodou, Cuban Yoruba, and Bahian Candomblé*. Chicago: University of Illinois Press.

de la Fuente, Alejandro. 2001. *A Nation for All: Race, Inequality, and Politics in Twentieth-Century Cuba*. Chapel Hill: University of North Carolina Press.

Deren, Maya. 2004 [1953]. *Divine Horsemen: The Living Gods of Haiti*. New York: McPherson & Company.

Edwards, Gary, and John Mason. 1985. *Black Gods in the New World*. Brooklyn: Yoruba Theological Archministry.

Falola, Toyin, and Matt D. Childs (Editors). 2004. *The Yoruba Diaspora in the Atlantic World*. Bloomington: Indiana University Press.

Fernández Robaina, Tomás. 1994. *Hablen paleros y santeros*. Havana: Editorial Ciencias Sociales.

Friedman, Robert A. 1982. *Making an Abstract World Concrete: Knowledge, Competence, and Structural Dimensions of Performance among Batá Drummers in Santería*. PH.D. diss. Indiana University.

Gilroy, Paul. 1993. *The Black Atlantic: Modernity and Double Consciousness*.

Cambridge, Mass.: Harvard University Press.

Grele, Ronald (Editor). 1991. *Envelopes of Sound: The Art of Oral History*. New York: Praeger Paperbacks.

Hagedorn, Katherine J. 2001. *Divine Utterances: The Performance of Afro-Cuban Santería*. Washington, D.C.: Smithsonian Books.

hooks, bell. 1994. "In Our Glory: Photography and Black Life." In *Picturing Us: African American Identity in Photography*, ed. Deborah Willis. 43–54. New York: New Press.

Hurston, Zora Neale. 1990 [1938]. *Tell My Horse*. New York: Harper Perennial.

Johnson, Paul. C. 2007. *Diaspora Conversions: Black Carib Religion and the Recovery of Africa*. Berkeley: University of California Press.

Kapcia, Antoni. 2005. *Havana: The Making of Cuban Culture*. New York: Berg Press.

Klein, Debra L. 2007. *Yorùbá Bàtá Goes Global: Art, Culture Brokers, and Fans*. Chicago: University of Chicago Press.

Knight, Franklin W. 1970. *Slave Society in Cuba during the Nineteenth Century*. Madison: University of Wisconsin Press.

Lachatañeré, Rómulo. 1992 [1938]. *¡¡¡Oh, mío Yemayá!!!* Havana: Colecciones Echú Bi.

Levine, Barry B. 2009. *Reflections on a Puerto Rican Life, Benjy Lopez: A Picaresque Tale of Emigration and Return*. Princeton, N.J.: Markus Wiener Publishers.

Lovejoy, Henry B. 2009. "Drums of Şàngó: Batá Drum and the Symbolic Reestablishment of Oyo in Cuba, 1817–1867." In *Şàngó in Africa and the African Diaspora*, ed. Joel E. Tishken, Tóyìn Fálólá, and Akíntúndé Akínyemí. 284–310. Bloomington: Indiana University Press.

Marcuzzi, Michael David. 2005. *A Historical Study of the Ascendant Role of Bàtá drumming in Cuban Orìsà Worship.* PH.D. diss. York University.

Martínez, Ivan-Cesar. 2007. *The Open Wound: The Scourge of Racism in Cuba.* Kingston, Jamaica: Arawak Publishing.

Mason, John. 2006. *Ironti Aponni Meji: Remembrance of Two Flatterers.* Brooklyn: Yoruba Theological Archministry.

———. 1992. *Orin Orisa: Songs for Selected Heads.* Brooklyn: Yoruba Theological Archministry.

Mason, Michael Atwood. 2002. *Living Santería: Ritual Experiences in an Afro-Cuban Religion.* Washington, D.C.: Smithsonian Books.

Matory, James Lorand. 2005. *Black Atlantic Religions: Tradition, Transnationalism, and Matriarchy in the Afro-Brazilian Candomblé.* Princeton, N.J.: Princeton University Press.

———. 1999. "The English Professors of Brazil: On the Diasporic Roots of the Yoruba Nation." *Comparative Studies in Society and History,* 41.1 (January 1999), 72–103.

———. 1994. *Sex and the Empire That Is No More: Gender and the Politics of Metaphor in Oyo Yoruba Religion.* Minneapolis: University of Minnesota Press.

McAlister, Elizabeth. 2002. *Rara!: Vodou, Power, and Performance in Haiti and Its Diaspora.* Berkeley: University of California Press.

McBride, James. 1997. *The Color of Water: A Black Man's Tribute to his White Mother.* New York: Riverhead Trade.

Mesa-Lago, Carmelo. 1981. *The Economy of Socialist Cuba: A Two-Decade Appraisal.* Albuquerque: University of Mexico Press.

Miller, Ivor. 2009. *Voice of the Leopard: African Secret Societies in Cuba.* Jackson: University Press of Mississippi.

———. 2003. "Jesús Perez and the Transculturation of the Cuban Batá Drum." In *Diálogo,* 7 (Spring), 70–74.

Moore, Carlos. 1988. *Castro, the Blacks, and Africa.* Los Angeles: UCLA Center for African American Studies.

Moore, Robin D. 2006. *Music & Revolution: Cultural Change in Socialist Cuba.* Berkeley: University of California Press.

———. 1997. *Nationalizing Blackness: Afrocubanismo and Artistic Revolution in Havana, 1920–1940.* Pittsburgh: University of Pittsburgh Press.

Moreno, Isidro. 1999. "Festive Rituals, Religious Associations, and Ethnic Reaffirmation of Black Andalusians: Antecedents of the Black Confraternities and Cabildos in the Americas." In Muteba Rahier, *Representations of Blackness and the Performance of Identities.* 3–17. London: Bergin and Garvey Press.

Murphy, Joseph M. 1993. *Santería: African Spirits in America.* Boston: Beacon Press.

Nwankwo, Ifeoma K., and Mamadou Diouf (Editors). 2010. *Rhythms of the Afro-Atlantic World.* Ann Arbor: University of Michigan Press.

Orovio, Helio. 1992. *Diccionario de la música cubana.* Havana: Editorial Letras Cubanas.

Ortiz, Fernando. 1995 [1940]. *Cuban Counterpoint: Tobacco and Sugar.* Durham, N.C.: Duke University Press.

———. 1994 [1951]. *Los tambores batá de los yorubas.* Havana: Publicigraf.

———. 1993 [1951]. *La Africanía de la música folklórica de Cuba.* Havana: Editorial Letras Cubanas.

———. 1992 [1921]. *Los cabildos y fiestas afrocubanos del Día de Reyes.* Havana: Editorial de Ciencias Sociales.

Patterson, Tiffany Ruby, and Robin D. G. Kelley. 2000. "Unfinished Migrations: Reflections on the African Diaspora

and the Making of the Modern World."
In *African Studies Review*, 43.1 (April
2000), 11–45.

Pérez, Louis, Jr. 1983. *Cuba Between Em-*
pires, 1878–1902. Pittsburgh: University
of Pittsburgh Press.

Pryor, Andrea. 1999. "The House of Añá:
Women and Batá." *Center for Black Mu-*
sic Research Digest, 12.2, 6–8.

Ramos, Miguel. 2000. *The Empire Beats*
On: Oyo, Batá Drums, and Hegemony in
Nineteenth- Century Cuba. Master's the-
sis. Florida International University.

Rogozinski, Jan. 2000. *A Brief History of*
the Caribbean: From the Arawak and
Carib to the Present. New York: Plume.

Rolando, Gloria. 1991. *Forever Present, Og-*
gun. Documentary film. Video America
S.A.

Roy, Maya. 2002. *Cuban Music: From Son*
and Rumba to the Buena Vista Social
Club and Timba Cubana. Princeton,
N.J.: Markus Wiener Publishers.

Santiesteban, Argelio. 1997. *El habla popu-*
lar cubana de hoy. Havana: Editorial
Ciencias Sociales.

Sarduy, Pedro Pérez, and Jean Stubbs
(Editors). 2000. *Afro-Cuban Voices*
on Race and Identity in Contemporary
Cuba. Gainesville: University of Florida Press.

Sarusky, Jaime. 2005. *Grupo de Experi-*
mentación Sonora del ICAIC: Mito y Re-
alidad. Havana: Letras Cubanas.

Sayre, Elizabeth. 2000. "Cuban Batá
Drumming and Women Musicians: An
Open Question." *Center for Black Music*
Research Digest, 13.1, 12–15.

Scarpaci, Joseph L., Roberto Segre, and
Mario Coyula. 2002. *Havana: Two*
Faces of the Antillean Metropolis. Chapel
Hill: University of North Carolina
Press.

Scweitzer, Kenneth George. 2003. *Afro-*
Cuban Drum Aesthetics: Developing
Individual and Group Technique, Sound,
and Identity. PH.D. diss. University of
Maryland.

Summers, Bill. *Studies in Batá, Sacred*
Drum of the Yoruba: Havana to Matan-
zas. Self-published.

Summers, Bill, Neraldo Duran, Michael
Spiro, Kevin Repp, and Vanessa Lind-
berg. 2007. *Batá Rhythms from Matan-*
zas, Cuba: Transcriptions of the Oro
Seco. Kabiosile Publishers.

Tishken, Joel E., Tóyìn Fálolá, and
Akíntúndé Akínyemí (Editors). 2009.
Ṣàngó in Africa and the African Dias-
pora. Bloomington: Indiana University
Press.

Turner, Robert Brent. 2009. *Jazz Religion,*
the Second Line, and Black New Orleans.
Bloomington: Indiana University
Press.

Vaughan, Umi. 2012. *Rebel Dance, Ren-*
egade Stance: Timba Music and Black
Identity in Cuba. Ann Arbor: University
of Michigan Press.

———. 2005. "Shades of Race in Contemporary Cuba." *Journal of the Interna-*
tional Institute, 12.2 (Winter). Available
at: http://quod.lib.umich.edu/j/jii/
4750978.0012.211?rgn=main;view=
fulltext (accessed May 26, 2011).

Vélez, María Teresa. 2000. *Drumming for*
the Gods: The Life and Times of Felipe
García Villamil, Palero, Santero, and
Abakuá. Philadelphia: Temple University Press.

Wilson, Sule Greg. 1992. *The Drummer's*
Path: Moving Spirit with Ritual and
Traditional Drumming. Rochester, Vt.:
Destiny Books.

TRACK LIST

To listen to the audio tracks for *Carlos Aldama's Life in Batá* please access the following url: www.iupress.indiana.edu/f/9780253223784.

1 Alubanché (Intro)
2 Ewi Pamí (Changó)
3 Elekotó (Agayú)
4 Eni Obobo Soloju (Ochun)
5 Ñongo
6 Chachalokuafun

Oro Seco
7 Latopa
8 Ogun
9 Ochosi
10 Ibaloke
11 Inle
12 Iyakotá (Babaluayé)
13 Bariba Ogedema (Babaluayé)
14 Osain
15 Osun
16 Obatalá
17 Dadá
18 Oke
19 Agayú
20 Orula
21 Oricha Oko
22 Ibeji
23 Yewa
24 Yansan
25 Cheche Kururú (Ochun)
26 Alaro Yemayá
27 Obba
28 Odua
29 Bajuba Changó

30 Alubanché (Reprise)

Personnel: Carlos Aldama, Calvin Holmes, Rick Ananda, Taji Malik, and Umi Vaughan
Tracks 1, 4: Carlos iyá, Rick itótele, Umi okónkolo
Track 2: Carlos iyá, Taji itótele, Rick okónkolo
Track 3: Carlos iyá, Taji itótele, Calvin okónkolo
Tracks 7-29: Carlos iyá, Rick itótele, Calvin okónkolo
Track 30: Umi iyá, Calvin itótele, Rick okónkolo

Recorded, mixed, edited, and mastered at the Music and Performing Arts studios at California State University Monterey Bay by Dr. Drew Waters with co-producer and co-editor Dr. Umi Vaughan and artistic director Carlos Aldama March 20 and 21, 2010.

INDEX

Page numbers in *italics* refer to illustrations; page numbers in **bold** refer to terms appearing in the glossary. Relationships of family members to Carlos Aldama are given in parentheses.

Abakuá: Abakuá lodges, 9, 44, 49, 62, 78, 86–87, 159n35; Abakuá secret society, 9, 159n16, 160n19; Añá association with, 29; Carlos Aldama relationship with, 48–49, 86–87; Conjunto Folklórico and, 73; masquerade dance, 9, 32, 158n23; Matanzas as center for, 29–30, 32–33; migration to Cuba, 3–4; in Nigeria, 102–103; *plante* (ceremony), 46; sexuality and, 94

aberikulá (unconsecrated batá), 19–20, 130, **153–54**

Aceituno, Carlos, 147–48

Adofó, 44, 82, 160n23

African Diaspora: African American batá drummers, 99; drumming as symbol in, 147; in Europe, 104; fundamental connections of, 5; Western popular culture and, 39

Afro-Cubans: Afro-Cuban Arts Movement, 40; Afro-Cuban heritage, 3–5; Cuban military in Africa and, 71; Cuban Revolution effect on, 65, 69–71; political and cultural repression of, 39, 67–68; scholarship on, 39–40. *See also* Cuba; Lucumí; *and particular ethnicities*

Agayú rhythm, 124

Aguabella, Francisco, 2, 105, 133

Aguirre, Josefina (La Chiquitica), 60–61

Ajayí, Miguel, 44

Akilakpa. *See* Roche, Pablo

Ako Bi Añá (drums of Trinidad Torregosa), 82, 86–87

akpwon (designated singer), 22–23, **153**

Álaba (Cuba), 42

Alaro Yemayá rhythm, 59–60, 68–70, 116, 125–26, 142, 160n21 (chap. 2)

alcohol, 56, 58

Aldama, Alfonsito (brother), 79

Aldama, Antonio (brother), 86

Aldama, Carlos (Ọba Ḳọ́wé(i)'lù): as batá apprentice (of Jesús Pérez), xii, 43, 44, 48–50, 54, 60, 83, 89–91, *91*, 114–15, 136; on batá as dedication, 37, 64, 114–15, 140–42; as batá teacher, 9–10, 93–96, 110–11, *111*, *114*, 118, 140; drumming style of, 63–64; on folklorization, 67–70, 74, 160n22 (chap. 3); golden age of Lucumí culture and, 2, 41, 72–73; in *Historia de un ballet*, 76, *76*–77; Ọba Ḳọ́wé(i)'lù as title, xii–xiii; performing career of, 46–48, 52, 66, 74; personal life, xix–xx, 13, 41–42, 85–89, 159n12; photos, *76*, *92*, *106–107*, *111*, *114*, *139*, *141*, *151*; pre-Revolution experiences, 2; *sucio* performance and, 58–59, 130; swearing ceremony for, 54; as *tambolero*, 134–35; Yoruba heritage of, 42–43, 97, 102, 144–45

UMI VAUGHAN is omo Añá (sworn to the drum) and a priest of Ochun in the Santería religion. He is an artist and anthropologist who explores dance, creates photographs and performances, and publishes about African Diaspora culture. Vaughan is Assistant Professor of Africana Studies at California State University, Monterey Bay and author of *Rebel Dance, Renegade Stance: Timba Music and Black Identity in Cuba*. To learn more visit UmiArt.com.

CARLOS ALDAMA is also omo Añá and a priest of Changó in the Santería religion. He is a founding member of Conjunto Folklórico Nacional de Cuba and studied under its original musical director, Jesús Pérez, eventually serving as musical director himself. He has worked with the National Symphony of Cuba, playwright Roberto Blanco, Karl Marx Theatre director Alex Valdez, and has played with Adalberto Álvarez y su Son, Lázaro Ros and Olorun, and Gonzalo Rubalcaba. Aldama was born in Havana and lives in San Leandro, California.

This book was designed by Jamison Cockerham and
set in type by Tony Brewer at Indiana University Press
and printed by Edwards Brothers.

The text type is Arno, designed by Robert Slimbach, and
the display face is Ashley Script MT Std , designed by
Ashley Havindon, both issued by Adobe Systems, Inc.